New Directions for
Higher Education

Martin Kramer
EDITOR-IN-CHIEF

Building a Student Information System: Strategies for Success and Implications for Campus Policy Makers

Don Hossler
EDITOR

Number 136 • Winter 2006
Jossey-Bass
San Francisco

BUILDING A STUDENT INFORMATION SYSTEM: STRATEGIES FOR SUCCESS
AND IMPLICATIONS FOR CAMPUS POLICY MAKERS
Don Hossler (ed.)
New Directions for Higher Education, no. 136
Martin Kramer, Editor-in-Chief

Copyright © 2007 Wiley Periodicals, Inc., A Wiley Company. All rights reserved. No part of this publication may be reproduced in any form or by any means, except as permitted under sections 107 and 108 of the 1976 United States Copyright Act, without either the prior written permission of the publisher or authorization through the Copyright Clearance Center, 222 Rosewood Drive, Danvers, MA 01923; (978) 750-8400; fax (978) 646-8600. The copyright notice appearing at the bottom of the first page of a chapter in this journal indicates the copyright holder's consent that copies may be made for personal or internal use, or for personal or internal use of specific clients, on the condition that the copier pay for copying beyond that permitted by law. This consent does not extend to other kinds of copying, such as copying for general distribution, for advertising or promotional purposes, for creating collective works, or for resale. Such permission requests and other permission inquiries should be addressed to the Permissions Department, c/o John Wiley & Sons, Inc., 111 River Street, Hoboken, NJ 07030; (201) 748-6011, fax (201) 748-6008, www.wiley.com/go/permissions.

Microfilm copies of issues and articles are available in 16mm and 35mm, as well as microfiche in 105mm, through University Microfilms Inc., 300 North Zeeb Road, Ann Arbor, Michigan 48106-1346.

NEW DIRECTIONS FOR HIGHER EDUCATION (ISSN 0271-0560, electronic ISSN 1536-0741) is part of The Jossey-Bass Higher and Adult Education Series and is published quarterly by Wiley Subscription Services, Inc., A Wiley Company, at Jossey-Bass, 989 Market Street, San Francisco, California 94103-1741. Periodicals Postage Paid at San Francisco, California, and at additional mailing offices. POSTMASTER: Send address changes to New Directions for Higher Education, Jossey-Bass, 989 Market Street, San Francisco, California 94103-1741.

New Directions for Higher Education is indexed in Current Index to Journals in Education (ERIC); Higher Education Abstracts.

SUBSCRIPTIONS cost $80 for individuals and $195 for institutions, agencies, and libraries. See ordering information page at end of journal.

EDITORIAL CORRESPONDENCE should be sent to the Editor-in-Chief, Martin Kramer, 2807 Shasta Road, Berkeley, California 94708-2011.

Cover photograph © Digital Vision

www.josseybass.com

CONTENTS

EDITORS' NOTES 1
Don Hossler with Sarah Pape

1. Why All the Fuss About Information Systems? 7
or Information Systems as Golden Anchors in Higher Education
William Gorr, Don Hossler
This chapter explores the ascendancy of information systems in the scheme of institutional priorities and the strengths and weaknesses associated with vended and homegrown systems.

2. Costs of Enterprise Resource Planning System 21
Implementation—and Then Some
Evelyn R. Babey
Investments in enterprise resource planning systems are among the largest monetary and human resource investments made by higher education institutions.

3. Implementing Student Information Systems 35
Laurie Sullivan, Rebecca Porter
Careful planning, management, communication, and staffing can make the difference between successful and unsuccessful implementation of an ERP system.

4. Implementation Never Ends! The Postimplementation 53
Organizational and Operational Implications of ERP
Philip J. Goldstein
Successfully planning for ongoing support and maintenance may be more essential to realizing benefits from a technology investment than choosing the product with the most features.

5. The Impact of Implementing New Information Systems on 69
the Priorities, Management, and Allocation of Resources at
Colleges and Universities
Don Hossler
The hidden dimensions of leadership and of the costs associated with the implementation of new information systems should be carefully considered. They can help determine the short- and long-term success of new systems.

INDEX 77

THE WILEY BICENTENNIAL—KNOWLEDGE FOR GENERATIONS

Each generation has its unique needs and aspirations. When Charles Wiley first opened his small printing shop in lower Manhattan in 1807, it was a generation of boundless potential searching for an identity. And we were there, helping to define a new American literary tradition. Over half a century later, in the midst of the Second Industrial Revolution, it was a generation focused on building the future. Once again, we were there, supplying the critical scientific, technical, and engineering knowledge that helped frame the world. Throughout the 20th Century, and into the new millennium, nations began to reach out beyond their own borders and a new international community was born. Wiley was there, expanding its operations around the world to enable a global exchange of ideas, opinions, and know-how.

For 200 years, Wiley has been an integral part of each generation's journey, enabling the flow of information and understanding necessary to meet their needs and fulfill their aspirations. Today, bold new technologies are changing the way we live and learn. Wiley will be there, providing you the must-have knowledge you need to imagine new worlds, new possibilities, and new opportunities.

Generations come and go, but you can always count on Wiley to provide you the knowledge you need, when and where you need it!

WILLIAM J. PESCE
PRESIDENT AND CHIEF EXECUTIVE OFFICER

PETER BOOTH WILEY
CHAIRMAN OF THE BOARD

EDITORS' NOTES

During the past ten years, many middle and senior college administrators have found themselves involved in the implementation of new administrative information systems on their campuses. This is a task for which many of them had little training and were ill-prepared. We begin this volume on implementing information systems at colleges and universities with a brief story of how one of us, Don Hossler, became involved in the implementation of such a system.

> In the summer of 1999, the vice chancellor of budgetary affairs at Indiana University–Bloomington asked me if I would consider becoming the campus lead for the implementation of a new PeopleSoft® student information system (SIS). At the time of the request, I was serving as vice chancellor for enrollment services, so my involvement in the implementation of a new SIS was a sensible request. However, I declined. Over the years I had served on several universitywide steering committees on which I had learned of both the necessity and the complexities of implementing new systems. My actual response to my colleague, who was a well-regarded mathematician and also served as the de facto provost on a campus that did not have a provost, was, "I know enough about these implementations to know they are really big and really complicated. I already have one full-time job and have never aspired to know anything about student systems. Why would I want to get into the middle of this?" He smiled and said, "Wise man."
>
> My response held for about eight months. In the spring of 2000, he asked to meet with me again. Once again he asked the same question, but with more emphasis as he explained all the reasons why he wanted me to accept the assignment. As a faculty member for nearly two decades, I had been socialized, like all faculty members, to think of myself as an independent scholar with academic freedom. However, the administrator in me knew that when one of the senior campus leaders asks you to take on a task, twice, you either accept or step down. Thus began my five-year involvement in the implementation of a management information system at a complex, multicampus university.

This story frames the purpose of this volume, which is written to provide faculty members, middle managers, and senior-level college administrators involved in implementing enterprise resource planning systems (ERPs) with a perspective on the history and purposes of ERPs, the costs and processes associated with implementing these systems, and the issues associated

with the ongoing care and maintenance of systems once they are installed. We assume that the likely readers of this volume will have little previous experience in these areas yet have found themselves assigned to committees or to leadership roles in some aspect of an information system implementation. As with any project in which participants find themselves in unfamiliar territory, there is much to learn.

Involvement in an ERP implementation requires learning an entirely new vocabulary. Terms such as *vanilla, customizations, fit-gap,* and *vended solutions* are not part of the lexicon of most faculty and college and university administrators. Nevertheless, they are part of the lexicon of system implementation efforts. In order for these individuals to be effective as committee members or leaders in influencing the direction and success of an implementation project, it is imperative that they be able to participate fully in the discussions and to understand the processes involved in the implementation.

In any implementation of a new system, it is also important that the individuals guiding the process and making policy decisions come solely from the ranks of technical managers and functional offices such as human resources, financial affairs, and student services (admissions officers, bursars, financial aid officers, and registrars). Faculty members, academic administrators, and student affairs professionals should also be involved in implementation efforts to make sure that the new system supports academic policies in areas such as admissions and registration; that the human resource system captures the complexity of compensating faculty members who are paid from two different academic departments due to a joint appointment or who have a portion of their salary paid by an outside grant contract; and that financial policies serve the accounting needs of academic departments. Without strong representation from academic affairs and student affairs, both in leadership roles and on implementation advisory committees, the goal can easily shift to simply installing a system as inexpensively as possible with insufficient consideration about whether the new system supports key academic, human resource, and student-life policies and practices.

Administrators with experience in the implementation of ERP systems always assert that successful efforts need leadership and involvement from trusted senior faculty and academic administrators. Such individuals provide a degree of credibility within the larger campus community. In addition, they are likely to have a good sense of the faculty issues and student concerns that could galvanize opposition to an ERP implementation if not sufficiently addressed.

In the following chapters we move sequentially through the processes and issues encountered during an implementation. The first chapter, "Why All the Fuss About Information Systems? or Information Systems as Golden Anchors in Higher Education," by William Gorr and Don Hossler, provides a brief history of the use of information systems in postsecondary education. The chapter also discusses the strengths and weaknesses of the two primary modes of developing information systems for colleges and universities: (1) purchased or vended solutions and (2) homegrown or build-your-own systems. This chapter sets the context for all of the succeeding chapters.

In the second chapter, "Costs of Enterprise Resource Planning Implementation—and Then Some," Evelyn R. Babey looks at one of the most contentious issues surrounding new system implementation: the costs. She reviews all of the major cost drivers of implementation and draws special attention to the hidden and often overlooked costs—namely, the costs of training, backfill, and consultants.

Laurie Sullivan and Rebecca Porter, in the third chapter, "Implementing Student Information Systems," draw on their own experiences in implementing a new SIS to discuss the key stages and issues of an implementation process. These include such topics as leadership preparation, implementation methodologies, the development of a project plan, and staffing needs. Although the authors focus on SISs, their observations are equally useful for administrators and faculty members involved in implementing human resource or financial ERPs.

In Chapter Four, Philip J. Goldstein examines what happens after the completion of an ERP implementation. In "Implementation Never Ends! The Postimplementation Organizational and Operational Implications of ERP," he addresses the final critical part of any new system implementation—maintaining structural mechanisms to keep the system functioning effectively. As most implementations near their completion, there is a tendency for everyone, from senior campus leaders to hourly employees, working on the project implementation team to begin to relax in anticipation of *being done!* As Goldstein points out, however, ERP implementations are never really done. Due to the constant stream of system upgrades that deliver new functionalities while simultaneously affecting the way the system works, continuous project management and system maintenance are ongoing features of modern postsecondary information systems.

In the final chapter, "The Impact of Implementing New Information Systems on the Priorities, Management, and Allocation of Resources at Colleges and Universities," Don Hossler summarizes and highlights key considerations for those involved in ERP implementations and the ongoing care associated with them. He also discusses some of the less visible effects of implementations and their impacts on the budgeting priorities of institutions.

We close these notes with a list of definitions and terms contributed by Sarah Pape that newcomers to ERP implementation are likely to encounter:

Backfill Compensation given to an office whose experienced personnel have been assigned to the software installation as functional analysts; used to compensate staff for additional work or to provide temporary workers to help cover business responsibilities.

4 BUILDING A STUDENT INFORMATION SYSTEM

Build-your-own   Type of software application designed and developed by an institution for its own use; also referred to as *homegrown*.

Customizations   Changes or additions made to a software system to enable the provided processes to work according to the specific needs of the institution.

ERP   Enterprise resource planning; generally used as an abbreviation for *ERP system*, a software application that provides an integrated approach to business process solutions.

Financials or financial systems   Software that runs the accounting, payroll, and tax processes of an institution.

Fit-gap   An analysis or report that looks at a new software application, compares it to an existing business process, and notes where the software supports the process and where it does not.

Functional analyst   An employee who serves as liaison between the particular functional department in which he or she resides and the central information technology department. Functional analysts have the technical knowledge to perform the system management responsibilities assigned to functional units, and the functional knowledge of business processes to develop, set up, and maintain software to best meet the system needs of functional users.

Functional managers   The lead analysts and project managers in each processing area; responsible for the business process analysis.

Gaps   Areas in a software application where the functionality does not meet the needs of the business process.

Homegrown   A type of software application designed and developed by an institution for its own use; also referred to as *build-your-own*.

HRMS   Human resource management system; can also refer to Oracle's human resources application.

Interface   The method by which different software applications communicate information back and forth; also used to describe the way users interact with the software. In the context of this volume, interface refers to the pages and screens on which a user enters and reviews information in the software.

Legacy systems   Software applications used by institutions prior to the implementation of a new system.

Methodologies   Various implementation strategies for installing vended or homegrown ERPs. Individuals experienced in software implementations advise selecting an implementation methodology and using it consistently throughout the implementation.

Migration   The movement of data or programs from a development database to a production database.

Modification   Change made to the delivered software to meet the specific needs of the institution; generally used interchangeably with *customization*.

EDITORS' NOTES   5

Open source software   Software in which the source code (the programming of the application) is available to be licensed by others in such a way that they can use or change it to meet their own needs.

Patches and fixes   Repairs made to software, whether vended or homegrown, by technical and functional staff to enable the software to work as intended; installed on the system and released to various users in order to correct for discovered deficiencies.

Prototype   A business process designed to include all the components of how the business will be configured and how data will be processed. This could be a detailed set of documentation or a configuration or modification put into a development instance to test the business process solution.

Shadow system   Variant of *build-your-own*; refers to small software applications or databases developed by individual offices for their own use to accomplish tasks or track students, staff, or finances in ways that are not supported by the existing software program and information warehouses used campuswide.

SIS   Student information system; a student administration software application; also used by Indiana University to indicate Oracle's PeopleSoft® Enterprise Student Administration software.

Technical managers   The lead analysts and project managers in a technical area who are responsible for upgrade activities, maintenance, and the development of customizations and modifications.

Third-party products   Software applications used in conjunction with the primary software application or applications; also referred to as *bolt-ons*, meaning that they are not provided by the primary software vendor or designed to be included in a homegrown system.

Upgrades   New releases of a software application containing new functionality or fixes to software bugs (problems).

Vanilla   A vendor-designed software application that has been installed "as is," that is, without customizations or modifications.

Vended solutions   Software applications created and maintained by commercial companies for sale to others to meet business needs.

Workarounds   Solutions created to support processes that are not adequately provided for by the administrative software solution. Generally, workarounds include reports, add-on programs, and manual processing.

These terms illustrate project language that many nontechnical campus administrators and faculty members are likely to encounter if they find themselves involved in the implementation of an ERP. The ability of these individuals to guide the process effectively will in part be predicated on their ability to understand these terms so that they can participate in every phase of the implementation process. Readers will find many of these terms used throughout the rest of this volume; however, not all of the terms will be used, so this glossary can also be used as a stand-alone resource.

As with any published monograph or book, there are individuals who have provided assistance behind the scenes. We would like to offer special thanks to Dan Rogalski and Melanie Rago who helped provide organizational and editorial support.

Don Hossler
Editor
Sarah Pape
Coauthor of Editors' Notes

DON HOSSLER is professor of educational leadership and policy studies and director of Projects on Academic Success at Indiana University–Bloomington, where he has also served as vice chancellor for enrollment services for eight years.

SARAH PAPE is a lead analyst for student enrollment services at Indiana University–Bloomington, where she supports the student information system in the area of student records, control table maintenance, and testing coordination.

1

The importance and attention given to information systems are relatively new phenomena in the history of higher education. This chapter documents the ascendancy of information systems in the scheme of institutional priorities and considers the strengths and weaknesses associated with vended and homegrown systems.

Why All the Fuss About Information Systems? or Information Systems as Golden Anchors in Higher Education

William Gorr, Don Hossler

Every institution, including institutions of higher education, requires resources to exist and function. Corporations require materials, intellectual property rights, or services to sell or exchange. Colleges and universities require revenue, faculty, staff, and students in order to fulfill their missions of generating and disseminating knowledge and providing services to their communities. The more processes an organization performs, and the greater the amount of products or services it generates, the greater the demand for resource management. As colleges and universities have been asked to be more efficient and to manage resources more like businesses do, they have sought management tools to achieve these goals.

Perhaps the most visible demand for resource management tools among colleges and universities has been for administrative information systems, often referred to as enterprise resource planning (ERP) systems. An ERP system at a university or college typically includes functions such as a relational database and applications for managing admissions, registration, and financial aid; for managing human resources; and for budgeting and fiscal controls—all important activities for institutions of higher education. In recent years, publications ranging from the *Chronicle of Higher Education* to the *Greentree Gazette* have carried feature articles on administrative information systems covering vendors, costs, implementation, and uses.

There are several reasons for this focus on ERPs. Implementing ERPs can be a very large, visible, and expensive task. Some institutions have spent

more than $100 thousand to approximately $500 million on the acquisition and implementation of new systems (Hossler and Gorr, 2006). Other universities have attracted negative attention for the problems they encountered upon implementation. The large number of professional and support staff required to implement these systems is yet another reason that they have garnered so much attention. Administrative information systems have become essential tools, albeit expensive essential tools, serving as anchors to help institutions securely manage information essential for daily operations and add constancy in long-term planning.

Enterprise resource planning systems are important to colleges and universities for many reasons. In areas such as admissions and financial aid they can be critical to institutional competitiveness. The ability to customize communication in order to attract a sufficient number of tuition-paying students, the efficient use of campus financial aid to achieve enrollment goals, and the enrollment of a desired number of outstanding students or students of color are key institutional goals on many campuses. The registration and records systems sustain the core academic functions of colleges and universities. Human resource and financial systems sustain the fiscal and human resources of institutions. All of these areas are linked to effective resource controls for colleges and universities. These systems, though invisible to most administrators, faculty, students, alumni, and others, control much of the lifeblood of institutions of higher education.

In this chapter we set the stage for the chapters that follow. We start with the assumption that many college administrators and faculty are not well-versed in administrative information systems, and with discussion of why these systems have been the focus of so much attention in recent years. To provide definition and context, we examine the purposes of ERP systems and how their use in colleges and universities has evolved. We present an overview of the alternative to prepackaged ERP systems—build-your-own approaches by which institutions of higher education build their own systems or by which groups of campuses come together to develop a shared set of systems. After outlining the alternatives for campus information systems, we also look at the effects of Y2K and how a convergence of factors created an impetus to replace many existing information systems at college and university campuses around the country in a relatively short period. We close this chapter with a comparison of the benefits and liabilities for campuses that might consider purchasing such systems from a vendor or building a system in-house with their own staff. Most of the examples in this chapter are drawn from our experiences and studies of student information systems (admissions, financial aid, registration and records, and student financial and bursar functions), but many of the organizational change and cost issues raised in this chapter are also applicable to other administrative ERPs used for human resources and financial management.

The Emergence of Computer-Based Resource Management Systems

Most faculty members and administrators are unaware of the extent to which computerized information systems have become the foundation for the management of colleges and universities. As a result, many have been surprised by the costs and complexities associated with the acquisition of new resource management systems or institutional efforts to develop a new generation of homegrown information systems. To frame the challenges that administrators face with respect to buying or building information systems, it is helpful to look at how development of these systems has evolved over the past fifty years.

Mainframe computers in the 1960s became the mainstay of corporations for financial and inventory management, providing separate systems to help manage and control resources. Similarly, institutions of higher education began to rely on information systems in the late 1960s, and on student information, human resource, and financial systems in the 1970s. Like for-profit and other nonprofit organizations, universities have become increasingly reliant with every passing year on embedded information infrastructure (the hardware used to interconnect computers and users of a specific software application).

In the 1960s, computer hardware vendors, most notably IBM, furnished software packages with their hardware—utilities that could be used to record, access, store, and sort data (Campbell-Kelly, 2003). Institutions then employed programmers or contracted with a programming services company to develop their own programs, often employing the hardware vendor's software packages, to help automate the typical business processes of the institution (such as payroll, accounting, and human resource management). Over time, the software developed was tailored to incorporate the institution's business rule. Rarely, however, did these software applications process and exchange data with other parts or applications of the system that relied on the same information (Campbell-Kelly, 2003).

During this period, institutions cultivated groups of functional users who would experiment with how they could use automation and how they could use provided system utilities to manage and manipulate data associated with their functional area. Often these teams would cobble together procedures and products that would improve the effectiveness and efficiency of record keeping and resource accountability. Personnel associated with initial software development efforts gained expertise through trial and error as they worked to engineer software solutions for emerging functional requirements. The early impetus for developing software products was due to the lack of developed products available in the marketplace. If the institution did not devote the required resources to developing routines to store, manipulate, and report resource information, then it would not have the required products.

The concept of a software package evolved gradually during the first half of the 1960s. At first, prepackaged software was a technological response by computer manufacturers to a changing environment in which the number of computers was increasing faster than colleges and universities could add programmers. Prepackaged software was the most expeditious way to alleviate the programming bottleneck (Campbell-Kelly, 2003). These new software packages enabled universities to use these developed utilities to process and store data.

Universities employed computers to help manage business processes. To add desired functionality, they bought developed software products to manage registration and other central administrative functions. In this instance, a software product is a program that requires little or no customization to provide the specified functionality—and the vendor is contractually obligated to provide training, documentation, and after-sale service (Campbell-Kelly, 2003). As new software products were introduced, however, software vendors began to market their products aggressively. Because of the cost and complexity of these new systems, financial managers changed their definitions and began to classify them as capital goods rather than as consumable products. At the same time, a new class of costs incurred by businesses and institutions of higher education emerged—the cost of software license fees. Similar to electricity and other utilities, the payment of license fees soon became a recurring cost, another expense required in order to keep the campus's infrastructure operational.

Although these systems met many of the needs of colleges and universities, there was continued dissatisfaction with the shortcomings of separate, independent systems, which did not enable easy exchange of data between them. As a result, vendors began to develop and market relational database systems and enterprise resource management systems. These new systems provided an integrated platform for many administrative services, including financials, human resources, and student services. ERP systems are predominantly intra-enterprise focused and provide, at least in theory, seamless integration of processes across functional areas, with improved workflow, standardization of various business practices, improved order management, accurate accounting of inventory, and up-to-date operational data (Bendoly, Soni, and Venkataramanan, 2004). ERP systems on campuses can track and integrate a multitude of processes and functions, as well as maintain accurate accounting of students, faculty, and staff. At the system level, at the very least, enterprise systems help organizations eliminate redundant data in information systems, standardize user interfaces, and approach data standardization.

Y2K: The Impetus for Change

Comprehensive and integrated ERPs might not have garnered the attention they have in the last ten years if it were not for the anticipated arrival of the twenty-first century and the Y2K problem. It is possible that if not for Y2K the use of resource management systems in the marketplace would have increased more slowly and thus had a lower profile among college and university administrators. However, in the late 1990s campus administrators became aware that their invisible, ubiquitous, but vital information systems were at risk because they might not function when campuses entered the twenty-first century. As a result, for the first time large numbers of colleges and universities took a comprehensive look at their mix of homegrown and vended systems and asked fundamental questions about their viability. They were forced to ask whether they could upgrade their current systems that were either homegrown or highly customized vended products, or whether they should purchase new ERP systems that held the promise of placing all of their administrative information systems on one technology platform.

In asking these questions, most institutions of higher education were raising concerns that had not been systematically addressed before. University administrators were faced with significant decisions that would affect how they managed their institutions—decisions that would precipitate other organizational changes. Information systems were now an integral part of the university infrastructure, and although these systems were designed to help improve effectiveness, institutions were woefully reliant on limited resources to evolve them in order to provide the support expected by students, faculty, and staff. In many instances, institutions were in the position of considering major changes in these systems for the first time since they had been developed. This lack of experience explains many of the problems that have been encountered as institutions of higher education have worked through the complex issues associated with enhancing or replacing their information systems. They have gone through a set of changes in which they had little experience.

Concerns about Y2K created unique opportunities for the vendors of ERPs. Typically, information systems, especially student information systems, are not one of the most pressing concerns of trustees, presidents, chancellors, provosts, and chief financial officers. The risks associated with not responding aggressively to replace aging systems and having them fail at 12:00 A.M. on January 1, 2000, however, resulted in a focus on information systems at the highest levels of colleges and universities. This risk also created an unprecedented marketing opportunity for the vendors of resource management systems. During the previous three decades, the audience for vendors of hardware and software for higher education had been functional users such as registrars, financial aid directors, and programmers in information systems offices. Concerns about Y2K opened the door for senior executives from large vendors to make presentations not only to campus chief information officers but also to presidents, provosts, and chief financial officers. This confluence created the opportunity for these users to make decisions quickly and to make large commitments of campus resources in timeframes that are atypical for institutions of higher education. It is possible that different decisions might have been made if midlevel functional and technical staff had been more involved and if the decision-making processes had mirrored earlier decision-making patterns. In the next section of this chapter, however, we make it clear that university information systems have become so complex that there are no easy decisions when it comes to how to maintain such systems. Nevertheless, there is no question that Y2K created a convergence of events that helped to bring about rapid changes in the acquisition of ERPs and the requisite organizational changes that are necessary for the successful implementation of resource management systems.

Vended or Build-Your-Own ERPs: Myths and Realities

As we have already noted, some institutions have chosen to build their own resource management systems while others have elected to purchase commercial off-the-shelf ERPs. There are a spate of supporters and critics of both options. Advocates of build-your-own systems assert that homegrown systems permit colleges and universities to develop systems that meet the unique business process, curricular, and competitive needs of individual campuses. As institutions weigh the risks associated with developing systems in-house versus relying on outside expertise for data and application migration and implementation efforts, they see the potential to save significant resources while simultaneously creating their own information technology (IT) destiny. Institutions that opt to develop their own systems often explore the use of open source software—potentially bypassing the use of commercial products. The growing number of institutions attempting to develop and succeeding in developing their own systems, using and sharing developed open source software, enables institutions to save the recurring expenses associated with escalating licensing costs for commercial products. Migrating to an infrastructure based on open source software often increases the implementation risks undertaken by the institution. Whereas a commercial software partner shares in the risks of a contracted implementation, the onus for success for open source ventures lies solely with the university. Institutions that embark on this venture must invest a significant amount of resources during the development cycle to establish and foster cooperation with other developers; to discuss bugs, fixes, and needed refinements; and to share and exchange software. Institutional staff who develop and then maintain the institution's software will likely have a greater depth of knowledge about the software than will staff involved in the implementation of a commercial product. Consequently, they are likely to be more adept at customizing the software to meet evolving requirements.

Proponents of open source software and build-your-own solutions often note that open source software is free. While it is true that open source software does not have any licensing costs, it is not accurate to jump to the conclusion that institutions can implement open source software for free. The institution must devote significant amounts of intellectual capital to the development and implementation of a new system, as well as additional time to train the appropriate staff. Peter Siegel, chief information officer at the University of Illinois at Urbana-Champaign, states he is convinced that "academia is in a strong position to build open-source tools . . . especially in the areas most closely tied to faculty innovation, such as pedagogy, evaluation, research, collaboration and the dissemination of ideas" (2005, p. 21). The potential cost savings and opportunities to employ tools that potentially enhance learning and foster information sharing should be explored to the fullest extent. Institutions electing to embrace fully the option of open source software may forego licensing costs and can own, operate, and modify their software without any vendor encumbrances. The institutions will then be fully responsible for making all software changes and incorporating those changes into the operating system, all applications, and executable software. The IT staff will likely spend more time than will staff who employ vended solutions coordinating with users at other institutions—comparing notes on problems experienced, sharing software components, and discussing software components available in the open source arena.

Build-your-own solutions, including the use of open source software, offer institutions more control over system enhancements and upgrades than vended solutions and thus enable institutions to exert more control over the costs of ownership, which (theoretically) leads to savings. In addition, supporters of build-your-own approaches note that vended solutions often require the purchase of additional third-party vended products or customizations, thereby diminishing many of the benefits of ERP solutions. Advocates of contracted ERP solutions assert that vended products offer cutting-edge technological solutions, enabling colleges and universities to have all systems on a single technology platform and reducing the costs of ownership because the software vendor maintains the integrity of the underlying code. Vendors also provide regular software upgrades, including updates in areas such as changes in federal tax codes and financial aid regulations. Supporters of vended solutions suggest that student information systems have become so complicated that few institutions currently employ technical staff with the necessary skills to build their own systems; they also do not have sufficient funding to employ the extra staff required to maintain the systems over time.

Another significant benefit associated with vended products is the ability to acquire complex, state-of-the art enhancements that have been partially funded, tested, and implemented at other institutions. As the vendor responds to change requests from user institutions, all institutions that have purchased the software may reap the benefits of system enhancements when system upgrades are implemented.

In the next sections we take a critical look at the propositions offered by advocates of both approaches. It will quickly become evident that the strengths and weaknesses of both approaches are intertwined.

ERP Systems

Strengths. Commercial ERP systems have many desirable characteristics. The technology already embedded in new ERP systems offers a major cost-of-ownership advantage compared to many homegrown systems because it places all administrative systems in the same technological environment. As a result, different campus staffs can use the same standards and tools and have access to enhanced interoperability that enables more efficient system maintenance. In older build-your-own environments it is common to find, for example, that the records and registration system was written in COBOL, accessing a hierarchical database; the financial aid system was developed in FORTRAN, accessing flat files; and the admissions system was developed using a fourth-generation language (such as Pacbase or SQL), accessing a relational database. In addition, several other smaller support systems may be developed in Access, Powerbuilder, or Java, each adhering to different software standards and programming conventions. This requires institutions to attempt to enable these different applications and data repositories to communicate and exchange data in order to operate together effectively. Such efforts can be costly and require colleges and universities to retain staff with knowledge and expertise in all of the different programs, some of which are no longer fully supported technologically by the industry. ERP systems, on the other hand, all rest on the same technological platform. This is a significant advantage that facilitates training and retaining personnel with the requisite skills for system development and maintenance.

Another standard weakness of legacy systems, especially older homegrown systems, is that they often lack documentation for programmers and users. This means that as new staff are hired or as new programming is required it can be difficult to train new users or to change programming features. Several years ago one major university reached a point where it was almost unable to deliver student financial aid because there was only one programmer left who knew enough about the university's legacy system to make all the changes required when the federal government enacted several major changes in the federal financial aid policy. That programmer simply did not have enough time to get all of the programming changes made in a timely fashion and there was no documentation for other programmers to use to assist with this effort.

Administrative systems have become very complicated, and IT managers are constantly faced with the challenge of retaining enough trained staff to keep them operating effectively. Vended systems alleviate many of these problems. Vended ERP systems also typically provide better documentation for campus users. The IT staff does not need to have the same technical skill sets as they do for homegrown systems; true design and development activities are undertaken only by the vendor. Consequently, the institution does not have as great a need for staff to maintain the system. When campus users run into technical or functional problems, the vendor's call center has the required staff available to answer most questions, or it has ready access to technical experts to help resolve seemingly insurmountable problems. At the system level, at the very least, enterprise systems help organizations eliminate redundant data in information systems, standardize user interfaces, and approach data standardization. Enterprise systems also reduce the requirements for support staff to maintain and develop system enhancements—although support staff will still be involved with developing data products (such as reports).

A well-touted advantage of ERP systems is that the companies who create and market them have also established user groups to find optimal business solutions, workarounds, and customizations. Among colleges and universities, there are user groups that comprise technical and functional staff from the colleges and universities that have purchased the student, human resource, or financial system from a specific vendor. Higher education, unlike many for-profit businesses, has a history of sharing and collaboration among institutions. Thus, if one campus is running into a problem with its vended financial system, it can contact individuals on other campuses who are in the user group and ask them if they have had similar problems and learn about possible solutions to resolve those problems. User groups offer an important advantage for vended systems.

Another benefit of vended ERP systems is that they ensure that colleges and universities will stay current with their technology. Because the companies that produce ERP systems regularly release upgrades in both the technological platform and the functionality of their systems, institutions of higher education are less likely to have the kinds of problems they have had in the past when their homegrown legacy systems simply have no longer been adequate to do the important work of the campus.

A key advantage of adopting an ERP strategy is that it expedites the ability to get new system functionality in the hands of users. As new system features become technologically feasible, the vendor has the ability to marshal resources to provide systemwide enhancements that computer support staffs at other institutions do not have the training or expertise to implement. Typically, institutions elect to implement a skeleton version of the software, running in parallel with the legacy system, and then add functionality once users become familiar with the system. Operating two systems in parallel is costly in terms of resource requirements—space, equipment, and human resources. Although it does reduce risk, it often requires system users to duplicate efforts, working with both the old and new system. Incremental implementation does facilitate generating user buy-in to the new system, and it allows users to adapt to the new environment at a comfortable pace.

A final advantage of vended ERP systems is that once you buy a system, this creates an imperative to implement it. By this we mean that once senior administration has purchased a product, they perceive a strong need to install the new system and start accruing the benefits of the investment.

Often the implementation of a new system turns out to be more difficult and expensive than senior campus administrators imagined; nevertheless, the press to implement the new system is pervasive and tends to move an implementation forward.

In contrast, one of the problems with a build-your-own solution to administrative systems is that the costs of customized systems are high and such systems require several years to implement. The budget for building in-house systems can become an easy target for reductions and reallocation because no external contractual commitment is influencing the implementation. This budgetary erosion slowly and imperceptibly reduces the probability of a successful implementation. More than one college or university, after several years of work on homegrown solutions, has cancelled the project and lost the investment in this approach only to turn around and purchase a vended solution and start the implementation process all over again.

Weaknesses. A major weakness of vended solutions is that they never meet all needs for unique business practices, which leads to customizations or additional third-party products. Customizations and third-party products increase the long-term cost of ownership of ERP systems. In addition, some of the unique strengths of build-your-own systems provide competitive advantages over other institutions in areas such as new student recruitment that assist individual campuses in achieving their enrollment or revenue goals. Vended systems, because everyone initially has the same system, can actually cause colleges to become less competitive in their market niche by leveling the playing field. It is difficult to stand out from the crowd when everyone offers the same features.

Another key weakness lies in the area of cost control and the timeline for future enhancements. Universities with homegrown legacy systems have complete control over whether and when they want to develop enhancements that could make them more efficient or effective in achieving a desired goal. In ERP systems, campuses are tied to the enhancement and upgrade plans of the vendors. Local customizations at the campus level can be so expensive as to be prohibitive. On the other hand, ERP solutions can actually increase the number of functional staff in some areas because labor-saving solutions require customizations that are too costly. This is a key area that requires careful analysis when considering vended or homegrown solutions. Institutions may be forced to hire more functional staff to work around the shortcomings of vended solutions. The full costs of ownership, both functional and technical, should be evaluated.

Another weakness of ERPs is that, in a certain sense, they remove the budgetary discretion that comes with the deferred maintenance options found in build-your-own systems. Universities often have no choice but to implement upgrades, patches, and fixes that come with ERP systems. If they do not, they do not have long-term access to changes in income tax codes that are part of human resource systems or to the changes in federal financial aid policies that are part of financial aid modules. In effect this means that deferred maintenance in administrative information systems is no longer a relevant concept. This is because there are costs that go with implementing system upgrades that campus administrators will have to undertake. Once an ERP system is purchased, these kinds of costs are no longer discretionary. One of the risks we address in the closing sections of this chapter is that if senior administrators try to keep the costs of their ERP systems close to the costs of their legacy systems, because of the built-in costs of regular upgrades, they will inevitably try to reduce costs on the functional side of their information systems. In doing so, they may lose competitive advantages that could increase revenues or reduce expenditures in other key areas of the university.

Build-Your-Own and Legacy Systems

Strengths. To critique the case for campuses to build their own information systems in higher education, a brief historical perspective is useful. As institutions of higher education began to use computers to help various functional areas manage their resources better in the 1960s and 1970s, functional users in offices such as registration and records, human resources, and other areas began to develop and maintain their own systems. Users who knew the existing business rules and practices could apply that knowledge to the emergent systems they were developing. In this environment, functional users had the ability to make and test changes to the software quickly, enhancing the feeling of control over system development.

The software tools, procedural programming languages, and hardware used were independently selected by these same functional communities of developers, with little oversight from higher administration. Indeed, in most instances each functional area developed its own system, often on different technological platforms, using different programming logic and different business rules. These early systems were not designed to interact with each other to share data. As a result, those who developed, modified, and maintained these systems soon became highly skilled and gained expert power as they amassed a greater amount of knowledge relative to other members of their respective groups (Hughes, Ginnett, and Curphy, 2002). Consequently, as a result of the internal competition for control and resources, these first-generation legacy systems did assist users in the organization to perform their tasks effectively; however, they did not necessarily enhance performance with fewer personnel.

Understanding the early history of legacy systems is helpful in understanding one of the greatest strengths of legacy systems. Harrison and Walton (2002) note that in legacy systems most maintenance is done for changes in program functionality rather than for fault correction. As system maintainers sought to be responsive to users, over time the complexity of various legacy systems increased (as new capabilities were added and existing deficiencies were corrected). Software maintenance was typically performed to adapt to changes in the environment (to accommodate new data-reporting requirements or to prepare for a new release of the operating system) or in response to failures in processing. These observations point out one of the most powerful reasons that many campuses are attracted to build-your-own solutions. Legacy systems enable functional users to develop local solutions for new policies and procedures adopted by the institution.

For example, a unique curriculum or customized approach to student billing can be supported more readily through the customization of locally developed software than through vended software. Some external observers of higher education, and some campus administrators, fail to recognize that customizations like these can be part of the strategic advantage of home-grown, customized systems. A unique curriculum can be one of the elements that contribute to the prestige of a small college or highly ranked professional school. Complex student payment plans for expensive private institutions can be an integral part of the recruitment process because they help make it possible for families to afford to send their children to the institution.

The primary benefit of devoting resources to develop and mature in-house systems pertains in large measure to control. In a vended product, requesting the vendor to add certain enhancements may prove to be cost prohibitive or require the enhancement to fit into a queue with other changes by other institutional customers. Also, the cost for the vended system includes functionality that is not used. Essentially, the institution is forced to allocate resources for system features that are not required and to forgo other desired features. By developing its own system, the school has the ability to build a cadre of personnel with the skills and knowledge to maintain the system from cradle to grave—although the recurring costs of keeping a full complement of trained IT developers and maintainers may be prohibitive for many institutions.

Another hidden benefit of build-your-own systems can be that they provide more discretion to senior campus administrators regarding when they will choose to invest institutional resources in information systems. This can of course be a two-edged sword; like erecting buildings, choosing to defer maintenance and upgrades on software eventually leads to having to spend significant amounts of money to completely reengineer legacy systems or to purchase vended systems. Nevertheless, most campus administrators defer investments in buildings or software because they believe they have more pressing institutional concerns to address. We look at this issue again in the section on vended systems; however, at this point we simply note that the timelines on when to spend money for commercial information systems are not discretionary. Vendors support versions of their systems only for specific periods, often four to six years. After that, new tax laws, human resource regulations, or financial aid regulations no longer work as required in the older version. As a result, institutions are forced to invest in upgrades. Again we note that institutionally owned and developed

WHY ALL THE FUSS ABOUT INFORMATION SYSTEMS? 19

systems provide more discretion on the part of senior campus administrators about when they choose to invest in information systems.

Weaknesses. Despite their many strengths, institutionally owned and developed systems often have inherent weaknesses. First, these systems are usually noted for their lack of documentation and for the difficulty that system support personnel encounter when they attempt to migrate the applications to newer, more reliable hardware platforms (Rahgozar and Oroumchian, 2003). Also, the various systems supporting administrative operations in the institution usually require separate support staffs (or at least teams) so that the system maintainers can continue to be responsive to users' needs.

These aspects of legacy systems increase the need for skilled IT staff members. The more integral the information systems are to the performance of the institution's core mission, and the more often the system is used, the greater the amount of ongoing maintenance and support that is required (Harrison and Walton, 2002).

Maintaining a sufficient number of appropriate staff is an ongoing problem with institutionally owned and developed systems. Within a few years after a system is implemented, the original system designers and developers are likely to take on new responsibilities and often transition to different employment. Newly hired maintainers are then faced with the daunting challenge of adding functionality without compromising the existing capabilities of the system. Resources are rarely allocated to develop training plans and documentation for new programmers. Software maintenance consequently becomes increasingly difficult as the complexity of the system increases and as ready access to resident system experts wanes. Similar to the maintenance needs of other university infrastructure, the problems of supporting legacy software become increasingly difficult and expensive over time. As a result, as in the analogy we have already made to deferred maintenance in buildings, information systems can languish, become fragile and dated, and no longer effectively serve the needs of a campus. In some instances they can become so fragile that they fail, resulting in the institution not being able to issue payroll checks, award financial aid, or register students.

Another risk associated with the build-your-own option is that information systems have become very complex and require highly skilled software engineers and programmers. Hence these systems are costly to develop and typically take several years to build. As a result, senior campus executives have to be willing to set aside large sums of money over several years. Most university presidents or provosts do not find information systems a compelling institutional priority. Information systems are the equivalent of the plumbing or electrical system of a building. They are invisible and they should simply work. In this context, there is a risk that funds set aside for developing a new system will be reduced over time, making it impossible to develop the new system envisioned in the original plan or to allocate the

NEW DIRECTIONS FOR HIGHER EDUCATION • DOI: 10.1002/he

required funds if the original cost estimate was inaccurate. A slow erosion of funding can place the entire project at risk.

On the basis of this broad overview of ERP information systems and build-your-own systems and the issues associated with their selection and implementation, the next two chapters provide a more focused look at their costs and a discussion of the implementation process and the steps institutions must take to ensure successful implementation. Following these chapters, Chapter Four considers how best to prepare for the tasks to be done in a postimplementation institutional environment. When many campuses begin their implementation planning they do not give much thought to how different the university's information systems will be after implementation. For long-term success, this is an important consideration. The final chapter offers some thoughts about the impact that new systems, especially ERP systems, are having on the management and allocation of resources at colleges and universities.

References

Bendoly, E., Soni, A., and Venkataramanan, M. A. "Value Chain Resource Planning (VCRP): Adding Value with Systems Beyond the Enterprise." *Business Horizons,* 2004, 47(2), 79–86.

Campbell-Kelly, M. *From Airline Reservations to Sonic the Hedgehog: A History of the Software Industry.* Cambridge: MIT Press, 2003.

Harrison, M. S., and Walton, G. H. "Identifying High Maintenance Legacy Software." *Journal of Software Maintenance and Evolution: Research and Practice,* 2002, 14, 429–446.

Hossler, D., and Gorr, W. "Enterprise Systems." In D. Priest and E. St. John (eds.), *Privatizing Public Universities.* Bloomington: Indiana University Press, 2006.

Hughes, R. L., Ginnett, R. C., and Curphy, G. J. *Leadership: Enhancing the Lessons of Experience.* (4th ed.) New York: McGraw-Hill Irwin, 2002.

Rahgozar, M., and Oroumchian, F. "An Effective Strategy for Legacy Systems Evolution." *Journal of Software Maintenance and Evolution: Research and Practice,* 2003, 15, 325–344.

Siegel, P. M. "A Taste of Open Source: This CIO Says to Drink the Kool-Aid, but as Part of a Balanced Diet." *University Business,* Dec. 2005, 8(12), 21–22.

WILLIAM GORR *is a doctoral candidate in the higher education program at Indiana University–Bloomington. Prior to pursuing his doctoral studies, Bill served for twenty-three years in the U.S. Air Force, where he led software development and software migration projects for the Department of Defense and NATO. Presently he serves as training coordinator for the Department of Homeland Security in Indianapolis, Indiana.*

DON HOSSLER *is professor of educational leadership and policy studies and director of Projects on Academic Success at Indiana University–Bloomington, where he has also served as vice chancellor for enrollment services for eight years.*

2

According to any accounting method, ERP investments are among the largest single concentrated investments in dollars and human resources ever made by higher education in any area.

Costs of Enterprise Resource Planning System Implementation— and Then Some

Evelyn R. Babey

Institutions planning to implement an enterprise resource planning (ERP) system often fail to understand the total cost of ownership of such an undertaking. Total cost of ownership includes not only the implementation costs but acquisition and long-term ongoing support costs as well. It includes "all direct and indirect costs that might be associated with the life-cycle stages of an ERP project, including its implementation, operation, and eventual replacement" (West and Daigle, 2004, p. 3). For the sixth year in a row, college chief information officers have reported that ERP implementations cost more in human and financial resources than any other issue related to information technology (IT) (Dewey, DeBlois, and EDUCAUSE Current Issues Committee, 2006). An ERP implementation is not for the faint of heart. It involves a significant investment of resources: money, personnel, and time (Green, 2005).

This chapter focuses on the total cost of ownership of an ERP system from the preplanning and acquisition stages through implementation to postimplementation, ongoing support, maintenance, and replacement. It stresses the importance of building and funding a realistic ERP budget that includes a substantial contingency fund from the beginning of the process.

The chapter begins with definitions of some common, key ERP terms that should assist the reader in gaining a better understanding of total ERP costs.

The remainder of the chapter focuses on the component costs of an ERP implementation at each stage of the process, including preplanning and acquisition, implementation, and briefly, postimplementation costs, which are treated more fully in Chapter Four. The forgotten and hidden costs of implementation are also discussed.

Understanding the Terminology: A Key to ERP Planning and Implementation

Before beginning an in-depth analysis of the costs of implementing an ERP system, college stakeholders should understand some common terminology that they will repeatedly see in print and hear in conversation. It is difficult to build a case for an ERP system and a realistic budget if the terminology is not clearly understood by all parties involved. Key terms include the following:

- *Enterprise resource planning (ERP) system:* Software that provides computer system integration and support to all units and functions across an organization in a single system, thus eliminating the need for individual unit databases or systems.
- *Hardware and infrastructure:* Physical equipment, such as servers, personal computers, cabling, network and clustering switches, backup devices, storage devices, and disaster recovery devices, required for an implementation.
- *Software:* All programs, procedures, and routines associated with a computer system. System software controls the computer's internal functioning. Application software directs the computer to execute commands that complete processes and solve problems.
- *Licensing fees:* The cost of vendor licenses for software required for an ERP implementation. These are usually one-time fees.
- *Maintenance fees:* The cost of vendor support tools such as mailing list servers, help desks, updated documentation, user conferences, consultant support, and application of software patches. These are typically yearly fees and tend to increase on an annual basis.
- *Customization:* Modification of base system software (code) to meet a functional need that the baseline product cannot.
- *Backfill:* Additional staff hired or reassigned from other departments to replace key functional and technical staff assigned to the project because of their knowledge, skills, and abilities.
- *Communication plan:* An integrated approach using various media to keep all stakeholders informed during the ERP implementation project.
- *Consultants:* Third-party individuals who have expertise and experience in implementing ERP systems. They are hired to assist the project team in implementing the ERP system in the most efficient and effective way in the shortest amount of time.

What Does an ERP Implementation *Really* Cost?

An ERP implementation generally has three cost phases: acquisition, implementation, and postimplementation. To avoid cost surprises during any one of these phases, it is important for a college to develop an initial budget that provides funding for all the components of the three phases, from the initial planning through "going live" to postimplementation and yearly ongoing support and replacement. The budget should include a contingency figure that amounts to at least 10 percent of the total project budget. In truth, unexpected costs do occur, but they are usually minimal in terms of percentage of cost if the original implementation budget is realistically developed and funded.

Acquisition Costs—Sometimes Forgotten. A true ERP budget cannot omit early costs associated with the process of deciding whether or not to implement an ERP system. *Initial* planning and acquisition costs are a real part of ERP implementation costs and should be included in the budget. Most of these initial costs fall in the area of human resource expenses (people) due to the amount of time key staff must dedicate to carefully analyzing the need for an ERP system, making a decision to pursue the implementation, and then planning for it. Staff time commitment includes numerous meetings with campus stakeholders to determine whether implementing an ERP system is in the best interests of the institution and to gain buy-in. Staff time is also necessary to identify and review ERP systems available in the marketplace; this time factor includes discussion with other institutions about their experiences with different ERP systems, vendor demonstrations, and visits to selected institutions to see ERP systems in working environments.

Travel costs associated with visiting campuses that already have operating ERP systems and attendance at vendor user-group meetings or professional conferences are funded through the ERP budget, not through departmental budgets. These planning activities are important because they provide key stakeholders with an opportunity to speak with many people in one place who have implemented or are implementing an ERP system. The travel costs can be substantial, particularly if several of the key implementation team members make these trips.

Once the decision is made to go forward with an ERP implementation, writing the request for proposal (RFP) requires additional staff time. It is critical that the RFP be well thought out and comprehensive. Any important aspect or feature of the implementation that is necessary but left out of the RFP can result in problems during the implementation. Such problems may cost additional money and staff time because they may delay the vendor in implementing the system in the originally agreed-upon timeframe. For these reasons, allocating sufficient staff time to carefully analyze the responses to the RFP must be a planned cost.

A well-designed communication plan is another early essential component of an ERP implementation strategy that should be developed and ready for use as soon as the announcement is made that the campus is considering the implementation of an ERP system. A communication plan is an important factor in keeping stakeholders abreast of the implementation progress, timeline, goals, and milestones. The plan should include a variety of media approaches for reaching campus stakeholders, including weekly newsletters (both paper and online), Web sites, video demonstrations, brochures aimed at specific groups of stakeholders, and live, interactive progress meetings. The communication plan must also include a feedback mechanism for stakeholders to comment, ask questions, and receive quick responses. Unfortunately, the importance of a communication plan is often overlooked and the costs are often underestimated. Kvavik, commenting on his experiences at the University of Minnesota, stated, "Build a communications budget that is four times what you think you are going to need. Then double it! You then have the right amount" (Kvavik and Katz, 2002, p. 80).

Implementation Costs. Once the decision is made to implement an ERP system, the development of the implementation budget can begin in earnest. A realistically developed and funded implementation budget that covers all components and aspects of the project ensures as smooth a process as possible and lessens to some degree the stress an ERP implementation places on staff. An appropriate budget will minimize the surprises of unexpected costs and the abrupt search for funds to cover these costs. If the funds are not available, the project can be put in jeopardy or result in a less than satisfactory implementation. This section discusses the major cost components of an ERP system implementation.

One major cost, usually, is the cost of new hardware, including network infrastructure. The institution of higher education (IHE) should budget for at least three system environments: development, test, and production. Generally an IHE will purchase some combination of database servers, application servers, Web servers, disks, load-balancing switch, and storage and disaster recovery devices. New or additional personal computers may be needed. The amount of hardware a campus requires depends on the size of the institution, the number of users, how many system modules will be implemented, whether or not a portal is being implemented, and acceptable system response time. If third-party software is included in the initial implementation, additional servers will most likely be needed. The ERP vendor works closely with the IHE to "size" the system and to determine what configuration of hardware and infrastructure is necessary to meet the needs of the institution, particularly its performance requirements. Infrastructure costs could be substantial if a campus does not have an adequate and appropriate telecommunications network and bandwidth. Coaxial cabling, fiber optics, network devices, routers, wireless networks, an uninterruptible geology

COSTS OF ERP IMPLEMENTATION—AND THEN SOME   25

power supply, power sources and backup power sources, and air conditioning are just a few of the potential infrastructure costs.

A major reason an IHE decides to implement an ERP system is to improve services to all constituent groups. To meet this goal, IHEs must understand the relationships among hardware, network components, infrastructure, and the service solution they would like to achieve, and then budget appropriately. The more people there are who use the system on a daily basis, the more application servers will be needed. A quick response time requires more application servers, more memory, and a faster processor speed, among other components. To avoid system downtime, redundant database servers are needed to provide automatic backup when one server malfunctions. IHEs must balance the cost of additional hardware with how much they want the new system to improve client services and business processes.

Software licensing costs include the ERP vendor software package and any third-party software the IHE decides to include as part of the initial implementation. The ERP vendor software includes the functional software for human resources and student records as well as all the software components required to run the new system, including the database, system tools, operating systems, compilers, and network and integration software. Third-party software is often purchased to enhance the functionality of the system—for example, a classroom-scheduling product intended to improve the efficiency of classroom utilization for a student information system, or a facilities management product for a finance system. Each third-party product adds a separate cost item to the implementation budget. A third-party product may also require additional hardware, such as databases, operating systems, and so on. Adding third-party software and hardware usually requires an assessment of integration with the ERP software and hardware. A third-party product may extend the implementation timeframe, which also has associated cost factors.

Hardware and software maintenance fees can be substantial. Institutions that have been building their own systems tend to forget the ongoing software maintenance costs that are part of a vendor package. The majority of ERP vendors include a software maintenance cost component in their contracts. These maintenance costs generally vary between 18 and 24 percent of the initial licensing cost, depending on the level of maintenance the IHE requires. Software maintenance fees typically cover software patches, new releases, vendor help-desk support, user mailing list servers, and the right to attend a vendor's user conference. It is important to point out that most maintenance programs also include an annual escalator clause that allows for increases in costs. The maintenance fee becomes an ongoing support cost once the system is implemented.

Hardware maintenance fees are similar to software maintenance fees and cover many of the same support services that software maintenance

NEW DIRECTIONS FOR HIGHER EDUCATION • DOI: 10.1002/he

fees cover, for example, vendor help desk, user mailing list servers, and patches and upgrades to operating systems. In addition, IHEs should build in hardware replacement costs as part of the ongoing budget. The life cycle for most hardware is three years.

A third significant cost associated with implementing an ERP system is staffing. To fully staff a project an IHE must consider internal staff assigned to the project (some think of internal staff as an indirect budget cost), back-fill for these staff positions, and vendor or other outside consultants. The staffing needs of the implementation must be fully understood and proactive approaches to potential staffing problems must be taken.

Most decision-level administrators understand that their top functional and technical people should be assigned to the implementation project; however, they often fail to understand exactly how much of these individuals' time will be required to implement an ERP system. Many administrators fail to account for the value of that time and for the significant additional workload that is placed on staff during an implementation (Powell and Barry, 2005). Reporting on the University of Minnesota's ERP implementation, Kvavik and Katz (2002) stated, "We clearly underestimated the personnel resources required for implementation" (p. 45). Gonzaga University reported that its indirect costs more than doubled the cost of acquisition. The majority of these costs were in-house human resources devoted to implementing and migrating to the ERP (Powel and Barry, 2005). The average percentage of total ERP costs associated with in-house staff as reported in the 2004 EDUCAUSE Core Data Study was 19.6 percent. The percentage ranged from a high of 23 percent for doctoral institutions to a low of 17.8 percent for bachelor's institutions (Hawkins, Rudy, and Nicolich, 2004). IHEs also fail to consider to what degree ongoing services can be negatively affected when key staff members are assigned to an ERP project. The loss of services is considered by some to be an indirect cost of the implementation.

In failing to understand how much time key staff will spend on the project, IHEs also do not acknowledge that implementing a new system puts a tremendous amount of pressure on staff. This is particularly true of staff who hold key functional roles and whose knowledge and understanding of the institution are important factors in the success of the implementation and the smooth operation of their offices. In many instances these staff members are expected to participate fully in the implementation and to continue in their daily roles. They quickly become emotionally drained and physically exhausted. They get sick and, in short, burn out. Some decide to resign. Others remain but become ineffective workers due to their physical and or mental state. In essence, ERP implementations tend to have both a human resources toll as well as a monetary cost. If key staff members depart from the project due to physical illness, emotional stress, or other factors, the project is delayed, which further increases the cost of the implementation.

Building an implementation budget from the beginning that includes sufficient money to backfill key functional and technical roles with qualified backfill staff who are hired and trained before the implementation begins should alleviate much of the stress described in the preceding paragraph. The backfill staff carry out the daily responsibilities of staff directed full-time to the project. A budget that includes backfill funds recognizes the valuable contribution key staff can make to the implementation project before it begins.

If an IHE chooses not to backfill positions on the pretext that it is saving money, it probably will find it has a false savings. Staff can do only so much well, and once they burn out or if they leave in the middle of the project, replacing them costs money not only in terms of recruitment and training but also because of subsequent project delays. Services in key functional units can be disrupted or delayed, affecting customer service and satisfaction. In a competitive market, poor services can be a factor in current students leaving or new students choosing to go elsewhere. Alumni who cannot get a transcript mailed in a timely manner may think twice about contributing to the annual fund.

The third area of staffing necessary to an ERP implementation is the use of outside consultants. This is another area where IHEs tend to think they can successfully implement an ERP system without spending money. Often IHEs fail to understand the complexities of an implementation and thus fail to engage enough consultant time. What seems like a prudent decision at the beginning of the project becomes costly when new processes are not as efficient as expected because consultants were not available to help set up the optimal process. The learning curve for in-house staff to gain the expertise and skills a good consultant brings to an ERP implementation could add months or even years to an implementation timeline. It also means that the improved services a new system provides are delayed. At one institution with which I am familiar it was thought that the in-house programming staff could learn Oracle quickly enough to eliminate the need for an Oracle consultant with programming expertise. The learning curve was so great that after six months or so it was decided to bring in outside assistance to get the project timeline back on track.

Implementing the degree audit component of an ERP system is an additional area where an expert consultant can help save money. Degree audit modules are extremely complex and involve a steep learning curve. If the module is not set up properly, students can be granted a degree erroneously. Vendor consultants who are degree audit specialists can work with and train in-house staff to set up the module accurately to reflect the academic policies of the institution. These consultants can do the work most efficiently in a lot less time than a staff member who has only a beginner's understanding of how the degree audit system works. Another institution with which I am familiar hired a full-time consultant for almost two years to bring up the degree audit system.

Although expensive and at times difficult to manage, good consultants can be an invaluable asset to the timely success of an ERP implementation, and campuses should spend the money to get the expertise they need (Murphy, 2004). Consultants bring vendor implementation expertise and have firsthand experience with new versions, new releases, and patches, and the skill sets they bring to the project can help bring staff up-to-speed quickly. They are critical resources (Camp, 2004). Kvavik and Katz (2002) found that "institutions hired consultants primarily to support training, provide ongoing project support, and help with system selection. They derived benefits from consultants on the basis of their particular skills, which were used to fill gaps in existing staff skill sets" (p. 15).

A realistic budget plan that includes funds for functional and technical consulting, as needed, helps ensure a successful implementation, although these costs can be significant. Results of the 2004 EDUCAUSE Core Data study showed that consultant fees averaged 18.6 percent of ERP expenditures (Hawkins, Rudy, and Nicolich, 2004).

Most ERP vendors provide in-house functional and technical consulting help at additional cost. Also, a growing array of third-party independent consulting companies provides functional and technical implementation services. In some cases an institution may choose to purchase the services of vendor consultants for one part of the implementation and outside consultants for another part. Some campuses choose to bring in a third-party consulting company to implement and then operate the ERP system once it has gone live. The type of consulting arrangement an institution chooses has much to do with the skill sets of in-house staff, the ERP system they choose, and the resources available. Some vendors do not provide consultants but require IHEs to rely on a "partner" consulting organization. A more comprehensive discussion of the role of consultants in a successful implementation can be found in Chapter Three.

Implementing a new system without fully training all users is a waste of time and money, yet many institutions do not adequately fund an ongoing training program. Here we explore the importance of staff training and why more is generally better than less. Training project implementation staff on a new system is vital if the new system is to meet the institution's implementation objectives. Yet many IHEs report that they did not adequately budget for staff training. Kvavik and Katz (2002) found that training was the most underestimated budget item. Koch (2006) reports that "training expenses are high because workers almost invariably have to learn a new set of processes, not just a new software interface" (p. 5). Koch further advises, "Take whatever you have budgeted for ERP training and double or triple it upfront. It will be the best ERP investment you ever make" (p. 5). Vendor consultants usually provide hands-on training for key functional users and technical support staff. The cost of this training is usually included under consultant costs in the budget.

The training of end-user staff is another critical cost factor in an ERP implementation. Some IHEs opt for a train-the-trainer model for end-user training. In this model, training is generally carried out by key functional implementation team members who are fully trained during the implementation. As IHEs realize that training needs do not necessarily end, they are beginning to fund full-time, ongoing trainer positions. The trainer is then responsible for developing and implementing an end-user training program. An end-user training plan must be professionally delivered, well thought out, organized, and delivered just-in-time (Kvavik and Katz, 2002). End-user training can be hands-on in a classroom setting or it can be Web-based, using course management systems such as Web CT. In most cases it is a combination of these activities. Training materials, whether paper, computer-based, or Web-based, must be developed and delivered.

Hands-on training requires a properly set up and dedicated training laboratory for ongoing implementation training as well as postimplementation training. Usually these laboratories have twenty to thirty computer stations, an LCD projector, and a good-quality screen. Some institutions already have a computer laboratory that can be dedicated to implementation project use. If a computer laboratory is not available full-time for the life cycle of the project, the implementation budget should include funds to set up and maintain one.

Training is a never-ending cost of an ERP implementation and the postimplementation budget should reflect this fact. If resources are not devoted to training staff to function in the ERP environment, the system will not be used to its fullest potential and people will return to the homegrown shadow systems they developed over time to accomplish tasks that university systems would not. In these instances, anticipated business efficiencies will not occur. The average percentage of total ERP costs associated with training as reported in the 2004 EDUCAUSE Core Data Study was 7.8 percent. The percentage ranged from a high of 9.7 percent spent by baccalaureate institutions to a low of 6.1 percent by doctoral institutions (Hawkins, Rudy, and Nicolich, 2004).

Customization of vendor software generally adds significant cost to an ERP implementation, and it is a cost that will repeat itself every time there is a new release of the software. IHEs must carefully consider the implications of customizing vendor software. We now explore some of the pros and cons of customization.

ERP systems available to the higher education market today are complex, integrated systems that are developed and enhanced on the basis of the changing needs and expectations of clients as well as the new technology available. When IHEs begin their ERP system review process, they look for the system that best fits their business needs, with the intent that they will not customize the underlying software code. Customizing ERP software code is costly at implementation and continues to be costly every time a patch, fix, or new release of the current version, or a new version, is released. This is because the customized code has to be retrofitted in the new release and has to be tested. Retrofitting and testing take key staff time.

Customization is usually done for one of two reasons: it is believed either that the ERP baseline code does not meet what the IHE deems an important functional need or that customization will save the IHE time and possibly money. An example of the former is Cornell University's decision to retain the ability to report a median grade for each course on a student's transcript when it converted its homegrown student records system to PeopleSoft's® student records system. The initial estimate for this change was $25 to $30 thousand. The total cost of this change will be multiplied every time a new version of the software is released (Olsen, 2004). Other types of customization result in long-term savings to the institution, particularly if the customization saves staff time in processing some function. Indiana University modified the front end of the e-document module of its vendor software. This modification centralized the process to fit the university's business needs, speeding it up and saving staff time every time the process is done (McDevitt and Walsh, 2005).

Hawkins, Rudy, and Nicolich (2004) reported that 37.6 percent of the respondents to the 2004 EDUCAUSE Core Data Study stated that they had modified underlying code. Doctoral institutions were most likely to have made modifications (49.7 percent) and bachelor's institutions were least likely to have done so (14.7 percent). In addition to making code modifications, 82.7 percent of the respondents indicated that they had modified the system configuration, and 72.8 percent had modified external modules. Kvavik and Katz (2002) found that "customization was the primary reason for projects to go over time and budget" (p. 14). Even if an IHE begins planning for an ERP implementation with the mantra "no customization," it should, to be on the safe side, include some contingency funding for it.

IHEs quickly learn that existing staff roles and skill sets are not the roles and skill sets needed in the new, complex ERP environment. New functional and technical support roles are needed. The new support roles tend to require higher skill levels and expertise than many existing roles. This means they are more costly roles to fill. We now discuss new roles that most institutions will find they need to create to gain the most business benefit from the new ERP system.

As mentioned previously, to meet user training needs throughout the life cycle of the system, some institutions create full-time trainer positions rather than rely on ad hoc training or training carried out by someone who does not have professional training experience or expertise. In a similar vein, ERP systems bring an increased need for professional help desk support. Help desk professionals have the skills and expertise in the software and in the technology supporting the software to answer users' questions or assist users in finding a solution to a challenge. Specialist roles in report writing have also evolved. Most ERP systems deliver very few reports, leaving IHEs to develop their own. The more complex the institution, the more reports it tends to need.

The role of *system coordinator* is now found in many core functional offices. The coordinator is typically responsible for maintaining the integrity of the data in the system; assisting functional staff with system challenges; liaising among the functional office, IT, and other campus units; and working with IT staff to resolve system glitches while developing and maintaining a systems operations calendar. The *IT security officer* is another role increasingly found on many campuses, but particularly on campuses that have ERP systems. ERP databases store a large amount of confidential information, and security measures must be put in place and monitored to protect that information from falling into the wrong hands. Among other roles that have been created or that have a greater presence in the ERP environment are database administrators, software system engineers, systems analysts, application programmers, and disaster recovery experts.

Each ERP implementation project will likely carry with it some unique costs. There are a few that all institutions will incur to one degree or another. The cleanup of data on the existing systems, whether paper or computer, is one example. If there are paper systems, there will be data entry costs. Data conversion and migration can be time-consuming and costly. Much depends on how much data is being migrated and how easily it maps to the new system. Building and testing links between the ERP system and other university software and Web sites is often an underestimated cost (Kvavik and Katz, 2002).

Postimplementation Costs—Costs That Never End! An ERP implementation budget is increasingly referred to as a total cost of ownership budget because costs associated with the initial implementation do not go away once the initial implementation is live. Postimplementation costs cannot be forgotten because they are substantial. They become part of the campus's operating budget. Staffing costs are associated with every patch, fix, new release, or new version of the system. If any modification was made to the underlying code, the code has to be recreated every time a new release or version is installed. As mentioned previously, there are ongoing software costs (such as when a new database is released, upgrades are made to operating systems and networking systems, or new third-party software is installed). Additionally, there are ongoing hardware costs as hardware is upgraded or replaced, and there are yearly hardware and software maintenance fees.

Consulting fees continue as new releases and new versions of the software are implemented. As with the initial implementation, it is important to have consultants with expertise and experience to assist in these upgrades. If the initial implementation focused on the core functional products, implementing other modules or new third-party software will most likely incur some consultant costs. Training costs also continue as new staff, faculty, and students arrive on campus and as new releases and versions of the software are implemented. Part of ongoing training for functional users and technical staff is attendance at professional conferences, workshops, seminars, and vendor user-group meetings. These activities should be funded as ongoing ERP costs.

Summary

The decision to implement an ERP system is not made lightly. It is expensive, and it usually takes eighteen to twenty-four months to implement from the start of the process to when the first function goes live. A complete suite of functions going live can take three to four years, or more. This chapter emphasizes that if an IHE goes forward with an ERP implementation, it must budget sufficient funds from the beginning, including a contingency amount. The budget must include funds for the three project stages—acquisition, implementation, and postimplementation—as well as funds for ongoing support, maintenance, and replacement. Each stage has critical components that must be funded. For example, all stages have critical human resource costs. Attempting to implement an ERP system without sufficient funds will only lead to a less than effective or efficient outcome, and to unhappy stakeholders and customers. It is unlikely that the new system will meet business needs or improve business processes to the fullest extent possible.

References

Camp, J. "Integrated Information Systems for the Campus." *Syllabus*, 2004. Retrieved Nov. 3, 2005, from http://www.campustechnology.com/print.asp?ID=8865

Dewey, B. I., DeBlois, P. B., and EDUCAUSE Current Issues Committee. "Current IT Issues Survey Report, 2006." *EDUCAUSE Quarterly*, 2006, 2, 12–30.

Green, K. C. "Digital Tweed/Commentary: ROI Is Dead!" *Campus Technology*, 2005. Retrieved Nov. 3, 2005, from http://www.campustechnology.com/print.asp?ID=11684

Hawkins, B. L., Rudy, J. A., and Nicolich, R. *EDUCAUSE Core Data Services, Fiscal Year 2004 Summary Report.* Boulder, Colo.: EDUCAUSE Center for Applied Research, 2004.

Koch, C. "The ABCs of ERP." *CIO Enterprise Resource Planning Research Center*, 2006. Retrieved Apr. 21, 2006, from http://www.cio.com/research/erp/edit/erpbasics.html?action=print

Kvavik, R. B., and Katz, R. N. *The Promise and Performance of Enterprise Systems for Higher Education.* Boulder, Colo.: EDUCAUSE Center for Applied Research, 2002.

McDevitt, D., and Walsh, B. "ERP Customization: Is It Always a Bad Thing?" CUMREC Annual Conference, 2005. Retrieved Apr. 20, 2006, from http://www.educause.edu/ir/library/powerpoint/cmr0573.pps

Murphy, C. "ERP: The Once and Future King of Campus Computing." *Syllabus*, 2004. Retrieved Nov. 2, 2005, from http://campustechnology.com/article.asp?id=8868

Olsen, F. "Big Systems: Living with Fewer Customizations." *Chronicle of Higher Education*, Jan. 30, 2004, pp. B9–B10.

Powel, W. D., and Barry, J. "An ERP Post-Implementation Review: Planning for the Future by Looking Back." *EDUCAUSE Quarterly*, 2005, 3, 40–46.

West, R., and Daigle, S. L. *Total Cost of Ownership: A Strategic Tool for ERP Implementation.* Boulder, Colo.: EDUCAUSE Center for Applied Research, 2004.

EVELYN R. BABEY *is principal consultant for Registrar & Enrollment Services Consulting for Colleges & Universities (RESCCU), LLC. She most recently served in the capacity of dean of academic and student services for the Higher Colleges of Technology in the United Arab Emirates. Prior to establishing her independent consulting company, Babey served as assistant vice president for enrollment services and university registrar at Georgia State University and as university registrar at the University of California, Davis, as well as in registrar positions in colleges in the New York City area.*

Implementing an enterprise resource planning system is a complex undertaking. Careful planning, management, communication, and staffing can make the difference between a successful and unsuccessful implementation.

Implementing Student Information Systems

Laurie Sullivan, Rebecca Porter

Once the decision to implement a new student information system has been made and the selection of the product concluded, the implementation clock begins ticking. Successful implementations are characterized by careful, thorough planning coupled with creative and deliberative problem solving as the inevitable, unexpected roadblocks (or at least potholes and detours) appear.

Although many of the concepts discussed in this chapter would apply to institutions that have decided to build and customize their own system or systems, the bulk of the discussion focuses on the process of implementing vended products. In recent years, the majority of large-scale implementations for student information systems have used vended products due to the complexity and resource intensity of the build-your-own approach. While several institutions have engaged in preliminary contemplations of an open source approach to the components within a student information system, similar to the Sakai collaboration (www.sakaiproject.org) being pursued for course management systems and the Kuali collaboration (www.kuali.org) for financial systems, no known collaborations have reached the stage of finalization.

This chapter presents the staged process that is typically followed during an implementation. The information covers both technical and functional perspectives in an effort to provide an orientation on how an implementation proceeds and to describe the critical decisions that must occur. Although it is an overview, it should provide individuals contemplating an implementation initiative with a perspective that can guide

them through their individual projects. As reported by Pirani (2005, p. 2), "IT matters, but technology alone is not the answer. Successful process improvement requires strong leadership, staff engagement in process improvement efforts, measurement, and new technology."

Leadership Preparation

Among the earliest decisions that shape an implementation initiative is the determination of which administrative unit will lead the overall project. A variety of institutional factors establish whether project responsibility will reside with the university information technology office, with other functional departments, or with an organization created specifically for the implementation. Regardless of who has leadership responsibility for the implementation, the project governance or decision-making structure must consider the roles that all constituencies will play in making decisions. Trade-offs are required between the desirability of wide campus involvement to promote buy-in and incorporate broad perspectives and the continual need to make timely decisions in order to remain on schedule.

Assessment of organizational and staff readiness for transition to a new system will permit the planners to understand better the assets available and the barriers that must be addressed. Careful consideration must be given about whether structural organizational changes should occur prior to implementing enterprise resource planning (ERP) software. The implementation process provides the opportunity for, and sometimes requires, realigning responsibilities within offices. For example, some universities have merged aspects of the financial aid and bursar operations due to the highly integrated nature of the ERP software.

Additional consideration should be given to the support required postimplementation because this will influence decisions throughout the implementation process. If the support for maintaining the system and dealing with the subsequent software changes provided by the vendor will be managed centrally, the functions need to be identified and plans made to train organizational staff. If the support structure is to be decentralized by assigning responsibilities to existing functional offices, the involved offices must be given early notification to allow them to adapt their structure to absorb the responsibilities. Regardless of the decision to centralize or decentralize support functions, benefits will be gained by involving the staff in future support responsibilities during the implementation process.

Throughout the implementation period, the implementation's leadership will need to remind various groups about the reasons for implementing a new student information system. When difficulties occur, as they unquestionably will, longing for the legacy systems will arise. If those involved in leadership were not involved in making the initial decisions, they should develop a clear understanding of the fundamental reasons that a change was needed. Did the current system lack capacity to expand to meet the needs of the institution? Does the new system permit integration of information among offices that was not previously available? Does the new system add features that were deemed essential but not available in the previous system? When pining for the good old days creeps into conversations, factual reminders are essential to refocus the discussions.

Along with understanding the reasons supporting the decision to implement, the implementation's leadership should thoroughly understand the dynamics that were involved in the decision-making process. Early identification of potential points of resistance permits the leadership to identify communication strategies for addressing areas of concern and to be aware of individuals who may add to complications during the implementation. As with any large project that has the potential to change fundamentally how an organization operates, continual communication strategies with multiple constituencies are crucial to the success of the implementation. Early in the process, mantras will need to be used, such as "No customizations of the software," "Keep it vanilla," "Use the software as delivered," or "This project will be completed on time, on budget, and within the planned scope." These fundamentals will shape subsequent discussions and decisions. At the same time, the implementation teams need to be empowered to explore paths that will ultimately better serve the institution by improving efficiency or preserving fundamental academic policies integral to the institution.

Critical Success Factor

The implementation's leadership must understand and carefully consider the factors that will ensure a successful implementation. Some of the key factors for success include the following:

- Visible executive sponsorship that empowers the implementation leadership to make definitive and timely decisions
- Utilizing a proven implementation methodology
- Ensuring that project team members possess appropriate skills and are available when needed
- Carefully managing expectations for the scope of the project
- Ensuring that funding is adequate
- Communication, communication, communication

Executive Sponsorship. The implementation of ERP software for any higher education organization affects the daily business operations of all users in the community, including executive management, department heads, staff, and students. A strong executive leadership that is engaged throughout the implementation and communicates effectively with the organization is critical. Leadership must be able to answer questions such as why the project is being undertaken, what the anticipated benefits are, and what the costs are. The significant change to business processes introduced during an ERP implementation affects all areas within the organization. Users must be given a realistic view of what to expect with the new system, and this information must be shared with the user community on a regular basis. The complexity of the implementation is shaped by a number of institutional characteristics. Does the implementation involve a single campus or is it a multicampus system implementation? How many different types of student populations must be considered? How many faculty and staff interact with the system? These elements not only influence the complexities with which the student information system must deal but also determine the type of decision-making process that must be employed.

Discussions are needed to determine which group or groups, individual or individuals are responsible for making the myriad day-to-day decisions concerning the project in order to stay on schedule. Decisions may need to go to different groups depending on the nature of the decision (such as academic policy, administration policy, or business procedures). Regardless of the group, the operational imperative must be timely decision making. Time is money and constant vigilance is needed during the implementation to remain within the cost projections.

Implementation Methodology. A key to success in implementing software is to plan and execute the project on the basis of a proven methodology. Unless project management expertise exists within your organization, it is often necessary to gain implementation methodology expertise through a software vendor or consulting firm. Universities that have developed and maintained their own legacy systems must learn new tools, methods, and development approaches to implement vended software solutions. Using a standard and consistent project implementation methodology to implement all product lines for software provides overall project structure, organization, and foundation for stepping through the never-ending set of activities and tasks that must be accomplished within a tight timeline. Using the same methodology for each project team (for example, human resource, finance, and student information) also makes it easier to share resources across product areas when necessary.

Project Staffing. Project team members with the required skill sets and business knowledge from each of the functional areas are essential; it is highly desirable to staff an implementation with full-time, project-dedicated team members (Rigelhof, 2003). The project team's leadership must also be given authority to make decisions in a timely manner. Countless issues involving business process design, project scope, timeline, gaps (differences between current business practices and delivered software functionality), and modifications will occur throughout the project, seemingly on a daily basis, and must be dealt with quickly in order for the implementation to remain on track. Those making the decisions need to be readily available. A process that enables feedback to be quickly solicited from key stakeholders in the university community needs to be developed in advance of the start of the project. Prolonged decision making increases the cost of the project and jeopardizes the timelines.

Very few ERP implementations have been accomplished without the use of highly specialized consulting resources. Consulting is a significant expenditure and needs to be adequately planned in order to avoid significant budget overruns. To prepare the budget for consulting needs, executive leadership should evaluate the university resources assigned to the project to understand the organizational strengths and weaknesses in both functional and technical areas. This assessment will help determine the approach the university should take to secure consulting resources to augment the skills and roles that are not prevalent within the university. For example, if the university has personnel with strong project management skills, an approach that augments specific key project team roles can be employed. Utilizing an implementation partner model for project management means that the consultant is providing the overall leadership to implement the software. It is wise to assign a university staff member to work hand in hand with the vendor to gain project management expertise. If the university has strong functional subject matter experts but does not have a large number of these experts, it may be necessary to hire additional staff from the outside to help manage each module to enable these scarce functional experts to work on content rather than on management. Even with effective in-house project leadership it is important to work with a vendor that has led successful implementations and has a solid set of procedures to follow.

When selecting consultants, consider the type of expertise needed for the project. Functional experts with work experience in a university setting prior to entering the consulting field may not always be knowledgeable from a system implementation perspective; however, they may provide good advice from a business operations perspective. Professional consultants whose expertise is primarily in managing implementation projects may not understand specific university business processes or the impact of the project on the institution. While both skills are helpful, it is important to understand which perspective a consultant brings to the table. When consultants from multiple firms are utilized, it is important that ground rules be established to determine which vendor's methodology is being used, how individuals should communicate, and what the supervisory relationships are.

Project Scope. The project scope identifies the list of deliverables that are part of the final project and is typically organized around the core functional modules that represent the major components of a student ERP product (such as admissions, financial aid, student advising, student financials, and student records). The project deliverables typically include an inventory of business processes, system processes, software functionality, reports, and modifications. The scope of what can be delivered during an ERP implementation is typically constrained by one or more of three factors: budget, staff resources, and timeline. A hydraulic principle comes into play among these factors. Limitations in the budget will expand the timeline. Accelerating the timeline will require increasing the staff resources dedicated to the implementation. Alternatively, if one or more of these variables are fixed, the project's leadership may need to scale back the scope. Expanding the scope during the project implementation will result in increases in one or more of the variables (that is, funding, resources, or time). While the principle of holding the line seems elementary, the forces that will push for expansions and customizations are pervasive in all implementations.

Funding. The ERP budget needs to be prepared and funding needs to be secured to get the project activities under way. Given the number of successful ERP implementations in higher education, ample data are available to assist universities with their implementation budget preparations. Chapter Two provides more information on ERP costs and budget development.

Communication Planning. Communication about the implementation is a critical element of any ERP project. Although the impact on the business process will not be fully understood until the project is well under way, it is critical to communicate the expectations for change management to the business community at the beginning of the project. In many cases, the complexity of ERP systems equates to the complexities in understanding how best to leverage new business practices. It may take several business cycles before functional offices experience the full efficiencies of new business processes.

It is essential to keep the university community informed about progress, schedules, scope, decisions, and problems while finding the right balance in the level of detail the project update communications should contain. Who is the audience that needs to be reached? Which medium and what frequency should be used for communications to various audiences? It is tempting to add the responsibility for communications to the duties of the project team members; however, communications are more effective and timely if a specific communications team is configured—even though the content will likely be drawn primarily from the individuals responsible for the implementation.

A good communication plan includes a two-part structure: an executive summary or overview to provide rapid delivery of information, and a detailed discussion offering a basic frequently-asked-questions section targeted at general audiences that simplifies content such as rollout schedule or timeline. The early communications should address the fundamental questions of the audiences and stakeholders: What does the implementation mean to me? When will I need to be prepared? And what will happen when the implementation hits the individual work station of each user? The messages should use a variety of formats and capitalize on the use of established distribution lists and regular communication channels such as brochures, campus mailings, Web sites, presentations, retreats, and town hall meetings. Web sites developed for project communication need to be updated frequently and targeted at specific audiences. Web sites that are used primarily by internal project team members are not effective for the casual university reader, who needs a brief summary containing fairly high-level information.

Building and Executing the Project Plan

Similar to peeling away the layers of an onion, building and executing a successful project plan requires multiple passes at gathering information, revisiting decisions and strategies made in the preplanning stages, and continual refinement of approaches as the project's leadership gains a better and clearer understanding of what it means to implement an ERP solution. After the project team is formed and high-level strategies are identified, the detailed project activities can proceed. The next sections of this chapter describe some of the key phases of the project: project governance, project organization and staffing, technology challenges, design and testing approaches, and finally, deployment to production.

Project Governance. Campuses need to determine the appropriate level of involvement for faculty, staff, and student constituents throughout the implementation of the project, and more important, they need to think ahead about the level of decision making the various constituents are to be given. Project governance committees need to be established with a well-defined mission statement (the clearly stated purpose of the group) so that the members of the committee understand their role. Will the committee be formed as a communication vehicle to provide regular status reports to others in the university? Will the committee members participate in making decisions about funding, resources, scope, timeline, and other elements? Will they serve in an advisory capacity when project members need to gather insights or feedback on specific issues and concerns? Faculty input is particularly needed on committees that discuss software differences that may affect academic policy, academic services to students, and other touch points of departmental processing and reporting. Inundating the faculty with minute implementation details, however, is not an effective use of their time. Depending on the faculty governance structure of the institution, it is important to identify any existing academic policies that cannot be supported by the vended software. If there are policies that would require extensive modifications or that cannot be accommodated, sufficient time will need to be incorporated for the appropriate faculty governance bodies to be consulted and for modifications in the policies to be made.

Project Organization and Staffing. A major activity of the planning process is organizing and staffing the project team. The project team's roles and responsibilities need to be identified. These roles may include project director, project manager, technical and functional managers, business analyst, trainers, change management agents, and others. Table 3.1 presents the typical responsibilities of the project team members. The project management team includes the leaders of the functional or business modules, technical managers, a project manager, and a project director. This team should meet on a weekly basis to discuss the overall project timelines, priorities, resources, issues, and management concerns as well as issues that affect more than one module area and that may require research, fit-gap analysis, prototyping, design, development, and testing.

Table 3.1. Typical Project Management Structure

Role	Responsibilities
Project director	Project oversight Resolve and evaluate project issues in areas of operating policy, staffing, project scope Facilitate external communication Acquire campus commitment for staffing Negotiate consulting engagements Manage project budget
Project manager	Develop and manage overall project plan Assist with development of module-level project plans Allocate resources Manage list of issues Establish overall project controls Manage day-to-day project work
Technical leads	Manage technical tasks Manage milestones Monitor progress on design, testing, report writing, and data conversion tasks
Functional leads	Provide direction for functional team members Identify fits and gaps Identify alternatives for gaps Lead prototyping effort Identify and track issues in their business area Responsible for change management within functional module area
Business analysts	Describe current business practices on basis of subject matter expertise Map business practices to the vended product functionality Guide team in making design decisions Assist with issue resolution Convert current operational procedures to work with new system

In addition to the project team, there should be a team of individuals responsible for implementing the new business processes within their respective campus or department operations. These individuals must work closely with the project team so that information about upcoming system changes can be communicated with local users in the department. The change management coordinator will assess the impact that the changes will have on daily procedures, assist with the modification of local practices and procedures as necessary, and identify training needs.

When functional resources are assigned full-time to project teams, it must be determined how the functional offices will cope with the loss of these key staff members. Considerations include backfill funding, shifting of responsibilities, and reduction of ancillary functions during the period of implementation. It is extremely difficult for project team members to split their time between project team responsibilities and home office responsibilities. This applies to both the technical staff supporting the legacy systems and the functional staff running legacy business operations.

Business analysts and technical staff assigned to ERP projects must have strong analytical skills. The skill set needed to accomplish home office responsibilities does not always match the skill set needed for project implementation activities. It is critical to assign knowledgeable individuals from the home offices to the project because the knowledge and understanding they bring both to the project and back home after the project are invaluable. Assigning to the project staff who are ill-suited for project implementation tasks increases the burden on and potential burnout of staff who have the skills to do the work. It is important to understand fully the skills that are needed to implement an ERP system and to understand the skills that exist within the university.

Technology Challenges. The technology organization has a series of questions to answer as project planning efforts begin. Decisions surrounding the hardware platform, operating systems, database technology, job scheduling, third-party tools (such as room management systems reporting products), and monitoring tools need to be evaluated. Depending on the ERP vendor, additional decisions may be needed to determine if products can be implemented in a single or separate database environment. The demands of a fast-paced implementation require several database environments to support all of the functional and technical prototyping, configuration, design, development, conversion, and testing activities. Staying current with application patches, updates, and fixes for all of the database environments used throughout the implementation cycle is a complicated task. The technical staff will need to keep these same environments current on the tools infrastructure, operating system, and database levels throughout the implementation. The institution may need to perform a major upgrade of the ERP software during the implementation cycle depending on the timeline of the project. A major upgrade is needed when the vendor releases a new version of the software that includes significant enhancements or updates to the technology components that require infrastructure changes. The vended student information system may not deliver all of the core functionality needed by the institution, which may necessitate partnerships with third-party vendors to provide missing functionality such as room management, Student and Exchange Visitor Information System (SEVIS) administration, address verification, and completion.

The technical team members who install the software and perform programming tasks need to be trained in the new technologies and skill sets. Holding onsite classes rather than sending staff offsite to attend training classes can be an effective way to reduce costs. It is important to gain insights and lessons learned by other universities to assist with capacity planning given the significant differences between the legacy system and ERP system needs. Estimating the concurrent number of users who will access the new system to determine overall capacity is challenging because the day-to-day business transactions that are processed do not match the processes in the old system.

Implementation Strategy. A key decision that needs attention once the project team members are in place involves the development of the project implementation strategy. This strategy identifies the timeline or schedule by which the new functionality is made available to the end users. The approach that works best for a given university depends on many factors, including the architecture of the legacy system and the amount of data to be converted, the scope of the work that will be implemented, the number of users affected, and the number of staff resources available to work on the project versus staff resources available in the home office to support the delivered functionality and the training schedules.

In a "big bang" implementation, all functionality in the system is turned on for use on the same date. The old legacy system is turned off and users work exclusively in the new system. Given the highly integrated nature of ERP systems, it is often difficult to turn on only some of the modules and features without additional programming work that provides interfaces between the legacy and the new system. An advantage to the big bang approach is that no short-term interfaces need to be developed because the old system will be turned off when the new system is turned on. A risk to the big bang approach is that all business processes go live on the same day. Because the scope of big bang implementations includes all business and system processes, there are many more potential failure points. In addition, the end users' needs for training and support are increased and may span a much wider degree of functionality. Hundreds, if not thousands, of new business processes are implemented as part of a new student ERP system; given the enormity of change, it is very difficult to train users on the entire new suite of processes and to support all of the users during the initial period when everyone is adjusting to the changes.

Table 3.2. Business Process Phased Implementation

Business Process	Timeframe
Set up student financial fees	Summer
Build course catalog and schedule of classes	Fall
Advise students for registration	Winter
Register students	Spring
Package financial aid for new and continuing students	Spring
Assess fees	Summer
Disburse financial aid	Summer/early fall
Produce class rosters	Early fall
Drop and add (class schedule adjustments), refunds	After classes start
Grades, transcripts, enrollment certification reporting	Late fall

A phased implementation strategy means that new functionality is phased in or delivered prior to being executed as part of the university business cycle. The example in Table 3.2 illustrates the new business processes that would be implemented in ten separate phases or releases throughout a one- to two-year timeframe.

One of the primary advantages of a phased implementation strategy is that end-user support and training are focused only on the scope of functionality or on features that are delivered for a particular release. The training can be limited to only the functionality delivered in that phase and can be delivered "just-in-time" or close to when the end users need to execute the functionality. Technically there are also fewer fail points. The downside to a phased implementation is that end users will be working in both the legacy and the new system environments. End users may have to perform dual data entry (entering the same data into both new and old systems) because not all interfaces can be programmatically developed. As the phased implementation progresses, there is a point at which the university will find it very difficult to quit and go back to the legacy system. One other downside to the phased strategy is that this approach does not easily support returning key staff to home offices to help with the new business processes as they are being phased in because the project team members need to be working on the next phase of the project implementation. Although it is difficult to staff the project team and the home office with experienced staff, universities that can backfill home office responsibilities for personnel assigned to the project are better prepared for the phased implementation strategy.

System or multicampus ERP implementations present unique challenges whether pursuing a phased or a big bang implementation strategy. The pressure to satisfy the diverse interests of campus administration, schools, and departments due to differences in business practices is extremely demanding. There may be different tuition and fee structures, student populations, and academic year dates, which make the overall coordination and communication more complex (Holland and Sullivan, 2005).

Development of the Project Plan. During this phase of the project, the team fully develops the project plan, project standards, communication plans, and training plans. On the technology side, the technical architecture, hardware capacity plans, and initial implementation environment begin to take shape. The fit-gap analysis is used to compare current business processes with the delivered software functionality to determine how well the vended product matches the existing system and where adjustments are required. New business requirements are inventoried and the delivered software is assessed to determine whether it meets these needs. The fit-gap analysis and prototyping activities determine the extent to which the software needs to be modified; this assessment is discussed in more detail shortly. After performing the fit-gap activities, the team will develop a detailed project work plan based on the targeted deployment schedule, available resources, and project scope. The plan will include activities, tasks, assignments, deliverables, and milestones.

Fit-Gap Assessment. Once the project team is trained and the environments are ready to support project teamwork, the fit-gap assessment work begins. This activity drills into the delivered software to determine how well it meets the needs of the institution. Identification of the gaps, or areas where the software does not meet the needs, will provide the list of potential modifications or customizations to the software. Prototyping is the phase of the project in which users can run business transactions and processes in the system. In prototyping the software and its business processes, it is much more meaningful to the end user if the software uses the institution's own data (such as academic calendar dates, majors and minors, degrees, class information, ethnicity types, and so on). The end users can more easily recognize and better understand how the software works if they see their department codes, degree codes, and major code values being used in business transactions. This step involves end users interacting with the new processes and provides a good mechanism to present findings to the university community.

Rules of Engagement for Gap Resolution. As universities deal with the functionality gaps between the delivered software and institutional policy and practice, decisions must be made regarding how to resolve the gaps. Most organizations are not financially able to make all desired software modifications and thus must work through a formal process to identify how gaps are to be resolved. Research on handling gaps may adhere to the following sequence of questions:

1. Implement an alternate vended product feature (workaround)?
2. Change university business processes?
3. Change university academic policy?

4. Change university organizational structure?
5. Develop a customized application or program?
6. Modify or customize the software?

If the software does not support academic policies and federal or local government regulatory requirements, it is likely that modification requests are necessary to satisfy the gaps. Administration of state financial aid awards is an area that typically will require modifications in the vended software.

Business Process Reengineering. A recent EDUCAUSE study explains that most universities seek to optimize the performance of their business processes in the student services area. "The benefits of process improvements are immediately evident to students and contribute greatly to their success and satisfaction" (Kvavik and Goldstein, 2005, p. 58). Universities will need to decide whether they want to reengineer business processes before, during, or after the ERP implementation. Business processes are more efficiently redesigned when business owners have a solid understanding of the system and its capabilities. After the system is in production, the team can shore up business processes that are not operating as efficiently as needed.

A certain degree of business process redesign is needed during the implementation as the project team becomes familiar with the way the new software works. The functional analysts must design new or revise existing business processes and procedures. Each process must be documented and reviewed with the end users. The end-user offices must reengineer business processes as they learn more about how the software works. Reengineering business processes is easier to accomplish in some project areas than in others. Multicampus system implementations require additional oversight to develop common business practices; different business processes for student information systems at each campus are difficult to support within a common student information system.

As the design of the business processes is solidified, the preparation of training materials begins. Ideally, templates and project documents used to gather user requirements can be turned into training materials. Training requires significant resources to develop content. There are never enough functional resources to do everything that needs to be done, and the same individuals are also needed to train, test, and prepare end-user documentation, all at the same time.

Design and Programming. During the design phase of the project, the software is readied for the system conversion and modification activities. Conversions, system interfaces, reports, and software customizations are designed and shared with the university community. The business analysts are at peak activity, solidifying the values that are coded into the configuration and setup tables, writing specifications for the modifications and reports, defining security requirements, and developing testing plans. Hundreds of control or code tables need to be designed and populated in the software.

A significant activity of the data conversion process is to prepare the data so it can be loaded into the new system from the legacy or source system. Legacy and vended software data structures and data elements do not always map well. If data are converted from multiple source systems, another step may be necessary to consolidate student records and determine which data elements contain the most accurate information. The team members assigned to the data conversion efforts develop a key understanding of the data model in the new system; this is the same understanding that is needed by those in the reporting community.

Testing. An overall testing strategy must be prepared to manage the testing activity for each release of the software. This is a key iterative activity that requires dedicated resources from the project team and from the larger university community. The project team must ensure that changes introduced through modifications work as expected. Individual team members representing each module are assigned the module-testing role and are responsible for identifying business processes to be tested as well as for determining what level of detail is required for the particular testing phase. A test plan documents the list of items that need to be tested and retested throughout the implementation. Testing is needed to confirm that day-to-day users can effectively complete their work activities within the system. Testing ensures that the business processes targeted for a specific release are running as designed, and validates that the delivered or modified code meets the functional requirements.

Beyond validating that the changes function correctly, testing provides a key opportunity to learn about the ERP software. Throughout the testing cycle, users are exposed to the application using real-life transaction scenarios. Testing can help identify product support issues that were introduced by the vendor. For example, when the vendor adds new functionality to the product or attempts to fix functionality that does not work properly, problems may be introduced that are discovered by the customers when they apply the new release of the software. If the specific release is not thoroughly tested prior to going live, then testing will occur in the production system and unpleasant consequences generated by initially unrecognized problems will need to be dealt with in an emergency fashion.

Reporting. The reporting environment purchased and delivered with the ERP system will likely not meet all of the institution's reporting needs. Most of the project team's resources are focused on getting the transactional system up and running, and the reporting needs take a back seat. The same business experts are needed to identify reporting needs and develop specifications for reports. Reports are critical to supporting the daily business operations by ensuring that the institution is complying with federal regulations, and to safeguarding data integrity. Once the operational needs are met, the institution can begin working on reports to support decision making.

Transition to Production. The final set of activities performed prior to the cutover to production includes running data conversions, establishing the production environments, testing, and evaluating the readiness of the user community to receive the new system. During this phase, testing continues to be a major focus. As described earlier, the system and performance testing takes place in this phase following the execution of the data conversions. The set of business and system processes that are moved into production will require ongoing management and support. A support plan is needed to identify the help desk staff and business experts who will provide answers to questions and issues that arise on a day-to-day basis and may involve research and analysis to troubleshoot specific problems. The support strategy will likely include a help desk and an electronic knowledge base where training materials, end-user documentation, and answers to frequently asked questions are easily accessible to those providing support. As mentioned earlier, training should be incorporated near the time the software functionality will be used in production, but not so far in advance that people forget what they learned before being required to use the information on a routine basis.

To evaluate the readiness of the user community for the release of the new software, it may be helpful to administer a survey or questionnaire that allows each office to determine whether they are adequately prepared for the new system. At this point it is also helpful to provide end users with reminders about training classes, help desk e-mail and phone numbers, and the procedure for reporting problems. Identifying the areas in which the user community needs to be ready can be accomplished by asking a set of questions that allows the supervisors as well as the project team to understand whether the end users are ready for the release or whether additional assistance is needed prior to going live. Table 3.3 presents examples of typical questions used to assess readiness for going live.

Going Live. During the deployment or going-live phase, the implementation of the new system moves into production. End-user training often continues after the system is implemented in production to coincide from a business perspective with the timeframe in which new processes need to run. During the upgrade, the production system may be unavailable to users for one or two days depending on the scope of the release during this period. Scheduling the go-live over a weekend typically provides the least interruption of services. The downtime for major implementations and upgrades may run four to seven days; this figure varies by installation and may depend on size of database, number of modules in production, scope of release, and so on. The final phase of testing is go-live testing

Table 3.3. Go-Live Readiness Assessment

	Yes/No	Comment
Training		
Have you and your staff attended the lab sessions or trainer practice sessions?		
Are all of your staff signed up for the end-user training sessions?		
Do you have plans for postimplementation training that you will provide to your staff?		
How do you plan to train new staff?		
Business Processes		
How are you planning to address initial backlogs in data entry?		
Have you considered reallocating some of your staff resources?		
Have you requested additional funding?		
Have you examined staff roles in your office and determined who will perform certain functions?		

(also known as production or cutover testing). Successful completion of this step confirms that the system is ready and can handle processes set to roll out for the deployment.

Conclusion

The implementation end-user support model must be put in place before going live with each release, and it is likely that additional staff will be needed early on to fill future support roles, particularly during a phased implementation. Despite the steps taken to train the user community, the amount of change is enormous, and the staff resources with core expertise will be called on to assist with back-office transaction processing, training, troubleshooting, setup changes, and general support regarding how the system functions following each deployment. This heightened level of support is needed just as the planning and development for the next release gets under way. Staffing is a critical component of any implementation, before, during, and after the project.

If you think there is really a conclusion to this process, you are sadly mistaken. The name of the implementation project will morph as will some of the work, but the process will remain an integral part of the institution as upgrades, modifications, and customizations are addressed. Then there is always the next version to consider . . .

References

Holland, N. B., and Sullivan, L. *Enterprise-Wide System Implementations at Multicampus Institutions.* Boulder, Colo.: EDUCAUSE Center for Applied Research, 2005.

Kvavik, R., and Goldstein, P. *Good Enough! IT Investment and Business Process Performance in Higher Education.* Boulder, Colo.: EDUCAUSE Center for Applied Research, 2005.

Pirani, J. A. *Good Enough! IT Investment and Business Process Performance in Higher Education Roadmap.* Boulder, Colo.: EDUCAUSE Center for Applied Research, 2005. Available at http://www.educause.edu/ir/library/pdf/ecar_so/ers/ers0504/ECM0504.pdf

Rigelhof, R. "ERP Implementation Best Practices: A Success Story." Paper presented at EDUCAUSE annual conference, Anaheim, Calif., Nov. 4–7, 2003.

LAURIE SULLIVAN *is director of the Student Information Systems division within Student Enrollment Services (SES) at Indiana University (IU). Prior to joining SES she held a variety of technology positions in the University Information Technology Services department, including project director for the Human Resource Management System and Student Information System PeopleSoft® implementations at IU. She is also serving her fifth year as a board member of the Higher Education User Group for PeopleSoft® users.*

REBECCA PORTER *is executive director of enrollment services and associate vice chancellor for student services at Indiana University–Purdue University Indianapolis.*

Planning for the ongoing support and maintenance that accompany implementation of new enterprise resource planning systems may be more essential to realizing benefit from a technology investment than choosing the product with the most features.

Implementation Never Ends! The Postimplementation Organizational and Operational Implications of ERP

Philip J. Goldstein

You can finally exhale. The implementation is over. The consultants have all gone home. The implementation team room has been converted back to its original use (such as a conference room or a supply trailer). The end users have been trained, all the interfaces are working, and you watch proudly as the first set of students is admitted using the new system. The hard work is over. The staff can go back to their old jobs. Right? Not so fast. In many ways, the important work has just begun.

Operating, maintaining, and upgrading a modern student information system (SIS) is not easy. Institutions are finding it challenging to absorb this work into existing organizations and staffing models. Gonzaga University reported in an article in *EDUCAUSE Quarterly* that more than half the costs of owning an enterprise resource planning (ERP) system stem from indirect costs such as the staff time required to operate and maintain the system (Powel and Barry, 2005). These costs far outweigh the initial outlay of funds to purchase hardware and software. However, properly executing the ongoing work of running a new system is critical to realizing the benefits that led to its adoption in the first place.

Should we be surprised by the ongoing workload to maintain a modern SIS? Probably not. After all, many institutions have moved to implement new systems because these systems offered the promise of capabilities that would grow and evolve as the institution's needs change. What has come as a surprise to most institutions is the level of effort it takes not only to

perform major upgrades but to keep pace with minor system changes as well after the implementation is over. In fact, many believe it takes two to three years after the implementation to understand a new system, fine-tune it, and realize its benefits.

A significant portion of the system's maintenance workload falls to the information technology (IT) department. In fact, IT departments typically experience an increase in staffing costs after the implementation of new finance, human resource, or student information systems. They typically must employ either more backfill staff to handle the ongoing maintenance of new technology or more technically skilled staff with higher compensation costs.

However, technology staff cannot maintain new systems alone. Just as the initial implementation team required a user-driven, collaborative effort with IT, so too does ongoing systems maintenance. This need has also caught most institutions by surprise. In fact, user departments typically see net increases in their staffing costs. Certainly efficiencies in processes may enable the organization to work with fewer people. However, this is often offset by the need for new kinds of positions to help manage the new system and to take advantage of its more extensive capabilities. As with technology, these new positions typically require greater skill levels and command higher compensation. This effect is not unique to SISs. The same postimplementation impacts are seen in other major systems, including finance and human resources.

To understand the phenomenon of continual implementation, it is useful to look back at where we have come from. Most institutions' legacy SISs were static. Changes were limited to annual financial aid regulatory updates or the addition of new reports. Occasionally the IT group would have the resources to add some new data fields or to create a new feature. Users participated in the governance of the new system and the occasional testing of a new feature but did not have to play a significant role in its day-to-day operation.

Today's SISs are much different. Vendors release updates, upgrades, and patches at a rapid pace. New features seem to become available every twelve to eighteen months (or sooner). Like a high-performance car that requires constant tuning, modern systems require frequent fine-tuning to maintain their alignment with evolving business processes and user needs. New systems also capture more information and make available better tools for users to do their own analyses. No longer do they need to wait for IT to develop a new report, but this change creates a new and different workload for some organizations.

The phenomenon of continuous implementation has had four broad impacts on institutions. It has

- Created a need for more active and integrated systems governance
- Necessitated a continual commitment to operations improvement
- Altered the traditional boundaries between IT and user areas in systems management
- Given rise to the need for a new user skill set

This chapter describes these impacts and identifies successful strategies that institutions can employ to manage them.

Governance

postimplementation governance

Most institutions have always had some form of SIS governance committee. During implementation of the new ERP system, most institutions form governance groups to set priorities, coordinate cross-functional issues, and make project decisions. Postimplementation operations require that these governance groups remain intact, active, and empowered.

The Need for Governance. The need for continuous, active governance is driven by three factors. Decisions must be made on a routine basis to allocate scarce resources, operations must be coordinated across disparate areas, and upgrades must be managed as if they were mini-implementation projects. Each of these factors is explored in detail in the paragraphs that follow.

The implementation of an SIS rarely delivers all the functionality that users ultimately want or need. The need to limit the project scope to contain risk and accommodate budget constraints is one reason. Another reason is the need to work with the system for a period to really understand its capabilities. This process enables an institution to make better decisions about which pieces of functionality it really needs. It is not unusual to see institutions with a backlog of work to be done after the initial implementation. Typically this work includes development of additional reports, activation of additional aspects of the system, and development or implementation of complementary technologies that work with the SIS, such as a scheduling module.

In all of these examples, the human resources required to create the additional capabilities are the same functional and technical staff who are occupied with operating the system. Most institutions have precious little discretionary capacity to do project work. A governance mechanism is needed to allocate this scarce resource and to establish priorities for enhancements and extensions of capability.

Coordinating operations across and among functions is another challenge that requires good postimplementation governance. In setting out to replace legacy SISs, higher education institutions have sought solutions that were more integrated than the old systems. Integration among the components of the SIS and, to a lesser extent, between the SIS and the human resource or finance system is viewed as a major driver of new implementations. Modern SISs have delivered integration. However, the byproduct of more integrated systems is an increased need to coordinate operations. Departments must share data fields and agree to common definitions of data elements. A simple example of this is the need to use address fields in a consistent way among offices. Integrated systems have accompanied a greater integration of business processes. Modern SISs have enabled such process integration as one-stop student services and Web self-services that tend to blur the boundaries that historically mapped business processes to individual functional departments. This too requires a greater level of coordination and governance than the previous systems required. What were once isolated changes that could be made independently by one function must now be carefully considered, tested, and vetted to make sure they work for all users.

The need for coordination does not stop at the doors of the student services offices. If the institution has also implemented a new finance, human resource, or advancement system, then there is a far greater degree of integration between those systems and the SIS as well. It is likely that all systems share basic biodemographic information about students and faculty. For example, an individual's primary and secondary address is shared across all components of the system. The student accounts system is likely to be tightly coupled to the financial system, and both systems are likely to hold many data fields and business processes in common. Likewise, there may be a greater coupling between the records module and the advancement system to track students' interests and activities as they transition to alumni status. The human resource system may share information and business processes with the SIS to manage staff who are also students and students who are also employees. This integration creates the need for more joint decision making. Just as the records office cannot change how it uses the system without considering the potential impact on other student services offices, the SIS governance group cannot make changes to the SIS without considering the impact of those changes on other enterprise systems. For example, the naming conventions of academic departments must be kept consistent between the records module and the human resource system, and the use of an address field by the admissions office may need to be coordinated with the users of the advancement system. Just as during the implementation, these ongoing adjustments need a place to be vetted, analyzed, and decided. Integrated systems require integrated governance.

Finally, the ongoing cycle of upgrades required to maintain a modern SIS also has driven the need for governance. Upgrades are in fact mini-implementation projects. As in a full implementation, priorities need to be set, policies and business practice changes need to be approved, and strong executive sponsorship is required to sustain institutional commitment. Fortunately, the issues are typically not as complex or numerous during an upgrade as during a full implementation. However, they are significant enough that they cannot be adequately addressed by individual managers acting only in their own unit's interest. Instead, a broader governance mechanism is required.

Effective Governance. To meet the challenges just described, successful institutions often elect to retain permanently the governance groups established for implementation. In SISs this typically requires at least a steering committee that represents the major stakeholders in student services. Representation is drawn from the major student service functions, including records, student accounts, financial aid, admissions, and advising. In larger institutions, the group may also include academic administrators from various schools or academic departments. In addition, there should be representation from the IT organization.

The governance of the SIS must also link to broader IT governance and priority setting at the institution. As discussed previously, the integrated nature of modern systems and the scarcity of resources require governance to span major systems as well as individual functions. In this regard, the SIS governance group may actually be a subcommittee of a larger administrative technology group or an overall IT committee.

The SIS governance body fills the role between the high-level strategy setting performed by an administrative or IT steering committee and the day-to-day decision making performed by functional managers in student services and IT managers responsible for the support of the SIS. The top-level IT governance function (IT steering committee) must address such questions as the following:

- What criteria should be used to select discretionary technology projects?
- What contractual or regulatory-driven maintenance must be performed on the administrative systems?
- What level of resources can be devoted to discretionary projects overall?
- What level of resources (people and dollars) can be allocated to the SIS this year?

Similarly, functional managers provide a layer of governance that ensures that day-to-day management of the SIS is performed effectively. Functional managers are responsible for decision making regarding the following:

- Day-to-day operations of the system
- Execution of discretionary technology projects
- Altering system configurations that affect single functional areas
- Approving the application of patches of limited scope

Between these two layers, a cross-functional SIS governance group is required to set the future strategy for the SIS and settle tactical questions that require coordination among multiple functions. At a strategic level, the SIS governance body should be empowered to set priorities for the implementation of new modules, to approve the development of additional modifications to the system (or the development of small programs to work with the SIS), and to request the purchase and integration of additional third-party products. The members of the governance body should serve as advocates to higher-level IT governance groups to request and obtain resources for the SIS. Finally, they should champion the effective use of the

SIS (and other support technologies) and lead efforts to extract maximum benefits from the investment in technology.

Tactically, the SIS governance group must coordinate decision making that crosses functional boundaries. The group should be empowered to approve changes to the configuration of the software that affect multiple functional areas. Maintaining the integrity of the data in the SIS is another important role for the SIS governance group. The group as a whole or through a subcommittee should be charged with approving any changes to the use of any system data fields that are shared across functional areas. Similarly, they should represent the system's users in broader discussions regarding the use of data fields that are shared by the SIS and other administrative applications.

Resource and schedule coordination is the final aspect of SIS governance. Maintaining a modern SIS requires the evaluation and implementation of frequent product upgrades. Some are limited in scope and affect mainly the technical support staff. Others can introduce new product functionality or significant changes to existing functionality. It is the role of the governance group to coordinate the upgrade process. Critical decisions include the following:

- When within the vendor-specified timeframe should the upgrade be performed?
- How does the upgrade need to be coordinated with other major activities that occupy the time of the student service professionals?
- If there is optional new functionality available in the upgrade, should it be deployed?
- Which staff will work on the upgrade and how will their time be backfilled in their home department?

The upgrade process is also a time to evaluate whether modifications that have been made to the system by the institution are still necessary. As institutions grow more familiar with the workings of a system, they can discover that modifications they previously thought were necessary can be supported by the base functionality in the system or accommodated through business process changes. The governance group must be accountable for making these decisions.

Multicampus Governance. Several institutions share SISs across multiple campuses. For example, the campuses within large, multicampus systems such as the State University of New York (SUNY) system, the California State (Cal State) system, and the University of North Carolina system have collaborated on the implementation or operation of their SISs. Similarly, some small, private colleges share an SIS with one another or with a larger university. For example, Drexel University operates an SIS for itself and Cabrini College.

The models of collaboration vary. All of the collaborators within a group use the same software, but not necessarily in identical ways. Some groups use the same software across multiple institutions or across campuses of the same institution. Some maintain separate configurations of software for each campus but operate them out of a shared IT organization. In general, the more tightly coupled the solution is, the greater the need for cross-institutional decision making.

These multicampus arrangements require the same type of governance group as that required by a single institution. In addition, institutions engaged in such collaboration may require discrete governance groups for each major student service function that spans campuses. For example, the overall student services group could have reporting to it separate subcommittees for financial aid, records, student accounts, admissions, and advising. These subcommittees would coordinate use of the SIS for their domain (that is, the financial aid module would be governed by the financial aid subcommittee) across campuses. Overall coordination would be provided by a single SIS steering committee with representation from each campus.

Alternatively, where each campus in the collaboration retains local autonomy and control of the SIS, the governance would more closely resemble that of a single campus implementation. This would be the case for a scenario such as the Cal State SIS. The Cal State system contracts with a single entity to host all of the campuses of the system. However, individual campuses control their own instance or copy of the software, which enables them to configure the setup uniquely to fit some of the specific needs of their campus. However, even in this less-integrated arrangement, there is a need for overall coordination of the SISs to make decisions about the timing of upgrades or the implementation of additional modifications.

Continual Operations Improvement

During implementation, project teams become well-versed in the traditional work phases of design, build, test, and implement. Significant effort is expended to design business processes that work well with the new technology, to build or configure the system to reflect the business practices and policies of the institution, and to test that configuration prior to implementation. This cycle does not end with the implementation. It is repeated even after the major implementation activities are completed. The need to fine-tune processes and the configuration of technology continually is another reason that implementation never ends.

Small Change, Big Impacts. Embedding technology in student service processes has enabled significant innovation and gains in efficiency. The last ten years have seen most institutions significantly increase the amount of technology they use in delivering student services. A consequence of this increased reliance on technology is that there is more to maintain. Each time an institution needs to change a business practice or policy, it must research how best to reflect that change in the configuration of its SIS. For example, the decision to add a new course or major will require the configuration of additional rules in the degree audit and records module of the new system. These configuration changes need to be researched, modeled, and tested before they can be put into effect.

The change just described is fairly contained and can likely be addressed by one or two individuals. More significant changes require more extensive effort. For example, an institution could decide to offer students the opportunity to preregister for classes a full semester early. If this practice was not anticipated during the implementation, the system must be reconfigured to adapt to a new set of procedures. The impact of the change could ripple through many parts of the system. For these more significant changes, an institution is in effect performing a mini-implementation project and must go back into the same mode of working they followed during their initial implementation effort. A team must be formed to research the following questions:

- Which aspects of the system are affected by the change?
- What tables or reports need to be modified?
- How does the configuration need to change to reflect the change in process?

Just as during the initial implementation, the changes that are being made need to be thoroughly tested before the institution can begin to use them.

Upgrades. Upgrades are another event that triggers the need to fine-tune processes and system configuration. An upgrade can bring with it new functionality that needs to be researched, configured, and tested. Sometimes an upgrade can also alter existing functionality. This requires the institution to revise its processes or alter some of its configuration choices. A major upgrade that alters many aspects of the system is also an opportunity to review previous configuration choices to make sure they are as effective as possible. In this regard, an upgrade can become an opportunity to take stock of how well the institution's business processes are functioning with the new system and to make changes that improve upon the set of choices made during the initial implementation. Vendors provide significant upgrades as frequently as every eighteen months. Smaller upgrades come out even more frequently. Therefore, the workload associated with upgrades is a significant component of continuous implementation.

The scope of change involved in an upgrade is often broad enough that the institution feels as though it is again implementing the system. Upgrades require the institution to take the time to research and understand how the new version of the software differs from the prior version. Vendors typically make available documentation that helps institutions perform this analysis.

Teams of functional and technical staff must spend time evaluating how the changes in the new version will affect the institution. Are there new ways to use the system to meet the needs of the institution? Are there completely new components available in the new version of the system that the institution may want to use? How will procedures need to change? Will users require retraining? These are the dimensions of the upgrade that must be evaluated and planned. The answer to each question will drive a set of tasks that must be completed as part of the upgrade process.

The changes involved during an upgrade are significant and must be tested prior to use. Even if all the software delivered by the vendor is free of defects, testing may reveal issues that have been created by the way the institution has configured the system. Thorough testing is certainly required to make sure that any new features available in the upgraded version are working properly. Finally, thorough testing will ensure that the new version of the system can still interface effectively with other software on campus.

Upgrades are also reminiscent of initial implementation work because they come with firm deadlines. These deadlines are driven by two factors. First, software vendors provide defined timeframes in which an upgrade must be accomplished. Failure to comply with these deadlines could void the software maintenance agreement with the vendor. Second, because upgrades consume so much staff time, they must be planned around day-to-day operations. SISs are especially challenging because there are few true slow periods throughout the year and often they are not shared by all the student services offices.

Finally, vendors release patches to their software on a monthly or weekly basis. Patches have a far narrower scope than an upgrade. Typically they affect just a portion of the system and are provided to address a deficiency found in the software code or to upgrade the technology. While much of the work of applying patches falls to the IT staff, some support from functional staff may be required. Functional staff may need to spend time evaluating the impact of the patch and advise IT whether it needs to be applied, or they may be called on to test the patch prior to its implementation.

Continuous Improvement. The workload of maintaining processes and system configuration is continual and significant. The effort to keep pace with vendor upgrades alone can stretch institutional resources thin. Though this work is difficult, its benefits are significant in that it provides institutions with the opportunity to expand and fine-tune how they are using technology. Few institutions can get all aspects of their implementation right the first time. A 2002 study of ERP implementations in higher education by the EDUCAUSE Center for Applied Research (ECAR) found that institutions experience a one- to two-year decline in productivity after their initial implementation (Kvavik and Katz, 2002). As staff members learn the new technology, the institution is positioned to see gains in productivity and satisfaction that surpass the preimplementation levels.

So, there is a payback to continuous implementation. Institutions that can retain their focus on continually fine-tuning their software and processes can achieve higher levels of effectiveness. The student services area appears to be realizing some of the benefits of this aspect of continual implementation. In 2005, ECAR did a follow-up of its 2002 ERP study to look at institutional satisfaction with the state of performance of business processes. The study, *Good Enough! IT Investment and Business Process Performance,* found that the institutions surveyed were most satisfied with their student service processes (Kvavik and Goldstein, 2005). However, achieving higher levels of process performance requires not only sustained effort but also a different kind of skill set among functional staff. This implication for staffing is explored in greater detail in the last section of this chapter.

Whose System Is It Anyway?

Another postimplementation impact that institutions experience is change in the division of responsibilities for system support between the IT department and other functional departments. As the preceding sections have described, the new world of continual implementation places significant responsibility on functional departments to participate in system management and support. This change is not unique to SISs; it is a byproduct of modern ERP systems. With such systems, much control is placed in the hands of nontechnical staff to access information and control the way the system operates.

Historical Division of Responsibility. Compared to modern ERP systems, the older legacy SISs changed little once they were implemented. Annual regulatory upgrades would be made to the system to reflect changes in financial aid policy, or an institution might make one or two modifications to the system. In the past, legacy systems were rarely controlled by tables or configuration values that could be easily changed by an end user; the knowledge and skills of a programmer were required to make even simple changes. Similarly, unless the institution had deployed a data warehouse or user-friendly reporting tools, extracting data from legacy SISs also required the skills of an IT professional.

As a result, users depended on the IT organization to maintain and enhance the SIS. It was not unusual in many legacy environments for IT staff to be responsible for programming reports, developing modifications, testing, and regulatory upgrades. If the institution introduced significant changes to its policies and procedures, an IT staff member would research how those changes rippled through the system. Users engaged in prioritizing needs for reports and modifications and helped to specify the changes they needed. A user with some technical skill might also develop some reports. However, at most institutions the responsibility for maintaining and operating the SIS was assigned to the IT organization.

Change Drivers. With modern ERP systems, the historical division of responsibilities is changing. Responsibility for maintaining the SIS no longer rests solely with the IT organization. Several factors are driving this change. First, the technology itself has changed. For example, tables largely control the operating systems that drive today's SISs. Once they are trained in the meaning of these setup tables and codes, non-IT professionals can understand how these tables and codes are used to control how the system functions. The implication is that an IT professional in a central IT department is no longer needed to modify a program whenever the institution needs to add a major, change an approval authority, or add an academic department. In fact, most changes to the system to support policy or process change can be made by a non-IT professional. Another technological change that has altered roles and responsibilities is related to reporting. Many institutions invested in new SISs to improve access to information. While the capability of SISs to improve access to information has proved to be somewhat limited, other complementary technologies have become available that make the extraction and manipulation of data much less complex than it used to be. As institutions have embraced data marts and warehouses, they have found that users of these data configurations can access information without assistance from an IT professional. At many institutions, the central IT department is now involved only in developing the most complex reports.

The second change driver has been the workload in central IT departments. Today, the resources of most IT departments are consumed by the effort to maintain existing technologies. Just as functional areas have been surprised by the ongoing workload of maintaining new systems, IT departments have been consumed by the effort required to maintain those systems technically. At the same time, the proliferation of technology use (driven in part by developments such as self-service for students) has given IT a new set of responsibilities in end-user support and IT security. A recent ECAR study of the state of IT funding found that 70 to 80 percent of the resources of most IT organizations are committed to maintaining existing technology (Goldstein, 2004). Very little time and money are available for enhancements or extensions of service. As a result, IT organizations have needed end-user departments to take on a larger role in system enhancement and maintenance.

The third change driver has been growth in the breadth of capability of SISs. The systems have become so robust that it is nearly impossible for an IT professional to learn the ins and outs of a single module, let alone of the whole system. Developing an understanding of the capabilities of a modern SIS requires the specialized knowledge and focus of a functional staff member in a student services office.

New Division of Roles and Responsibilities. As a result of these drivers, the responsibility for managing the SIS (or any ERP application) has shifted from being an IT-centered responsibility to a shared responsibility. Functional offices now play a significant role in the day-to-day management

Table 4.1. Division of Roles and Responsibilities for SIS Management

Central IT	Functional Offices	Shared Responsibility
Maintain hardware, operating systems, and databases	Maintain configuration of the software	Research new releases of the software
Develop modifications, custom applications, and interfaces to and from the student system	Run batch processes	Design new functionality
	Develop reports and queries	Troubleshoot complex issues
Migrate patches, upgrades, and changes into production (live) environment	Troubleshoot issues and errors encountered by users	Perform upgrades
Troubleshoot problems that stem from hardware, database, or interface issues	Test new system features and functions as needed	
	Train users	

of the system and are vital partners in cyclical maintenance activities such as upgrades. The IT organization's primary focus is on the infrastructure that surrounds the SIS. It maintains the hardware, databases, and operating systems on which the SIS runs. It develops and maintains interfaces, and creates specialized applications and some complex reports. On the other end, the functional areas are responsible for operating the application. They maintain the tables used to configure the system, develop commonly used reports and queries of the system, and execute major batch processes such as mailings. Table 4.1 presents a typical division of responsibility between central IT and the student services functional offices for the operation of an SIS.

A New Working Relationship

Modern information systems, including SISs, create a shared responsibility between the user department and the IT department. Just as during the initial implementation, troubleshooting complex problems, developing new functionality, and performing major upgrades requires both IT and functional staff. Close coordination and frequent communication must be maintained between user areas and the functional units to make sure these ongoing adjustments occur effectively.

Institutions find executing these shared responsibilities challenging, in part because their method of working with IT is changing. With legacy systems it was not unusual for each functional office in student services to have one or more dedicated programmers in the central IT department supporting their module. While these individuals did not report to the registrar or financial aid director per se, they were 100 percent focused on the needs and priorities of that user area. Over time, deep relationships developed and the IT professional came to understand the needs of that functional area quite well. Today, IT organizations are moving away from providing a dedicated programmer for each module of the SIS and toward a pooled model in which application developers are cross-trained in multiple aspects of the system.

The method of requesting that IT undertake a project is also changing. In the past, functional units had direct access to and control of the work priorities of their assigned programmer. At most institutions, this created an informal but effective mechanism for identifying and prioritizing projects. To manage their workload better, IT organizations are instituting more formal mechanisms for requesting assistance from IT. Requests must be made through the formal governance mechanisms described at the beginning of this chapter. Each request must be weighed and evaluated against competing proposals from other student service areas or other administrative offices on campus. Although this increased level of structure is often beneficial, it can have an unintended consequence of fracturing the relationship between IT and functional units. Leadership from both areas must work with their staffs to explain how structures are changing and why. The student services area must also keep in mind that these changes do not mean they have less ability to improve the system continuously. As discussed previously, users now have much more ability to effect change to the SIS directly, without the involvement of IT.

Absorbing these changes in responsibilities is also difficult if the functional departments have not anticipated them. Most student service organizations do not have the capacity to take on these responsibilities within their existing staffs. They lack either the required skill sets or sufficient numbers of staff, or both. The next section discusses the new kind of position emerging in functional areas to facilitate the system management responsibilities.

The Role of the Functional Analyst. The system management, continuous improvement, and cyclical maintenance responsibilities (such as upgrades) that are borne by functional departments are significant. Many departments have found it difficult to absorb these responsibilities within existing staff positions. For one thing, the skill sets are different. The system management responsibilities require a hybrid skill set that includes knowledge of the functional area, knowledge of technology, and consultative skills such as project management and process analysis. The workload is also too substantial to be performed by staffs that are also charged with delivering frontline services to students. There just is not enough time to do both jobs well.

Institutions are increasingly recognizing this problem and are creating new positions to focus on systems operations and management. The names of these positions vary. For the sake of simplicity, let's call this position *functional analyst*. The role of a functional analyst is much like that of a functional team leader (or external consultant) during the implementation phase. Functional analysts serve as translators among functional users, technical staff, and the software. They have sufficient technical knowledge to perform the system management responsibilities assigned to functional units, and sufficient functional knowledge to maintain the software in a way that meets the needs of users. Often they serve as the liaisons between the functional departments that employ them and the central IT organization. Typically their responsibilities include the following:

- Maintain system configuration tables.
- Run batch processes.
- Develop standard reports and queries.
- Troubleshoot software issues.
- Train end users.
- Develop specifications for new reports, modifications, and functionality.
- Test new functionalities.
- Maintain system user documentation.
- Identify process improvement opportunities.
- Maintain ancillary technology applications such as Web sites and imaging.

Creating functional analyst positions also magnifies the effectiveness of all end users of the system. The functional analysts provide expert understanding of the software system. Because they are located close to end users, they can provide immediate training, troubleshooting support, and assistance to staff in finding ways to use the SIS (and related technologies) as effectively as possible. They can instigate and facilitate continuous improvement projects and research potential new technology applications on behalf of all users. The presence of full-time analysts also gives the institution some highly productive staff it can draw on to serve as project resources during major initiatives such as an upgrade.

Organizing Functional Analysts. Determining the number of functional analysts an institution requires is not an exact science. Staffing needs depend in part on the complexity of the SIS software, the level of technology knowledge present in the student services staff, and the size of the institution. The backlog of process and reporting issues that are carried over from the initial implementation to the day-to-day operations is also a factor. Finally, the expected frequency and scale of vendor upgrades is also a determining factor. Most often, the number of analysts an institution has is a function of how many it can afford. Within reason, most institutions find that they can productively use as many analysts as they can afford to hire.

For large institutions, there is benefit to assigning one functional analyst to each of the four main student service functional offices. Some data-intensive areas such as records or admissions may benefit from having multiple analysts. For small organizations, it may be beneficial to share one or two analyst positions across multiple student service functions. As with any shared position, it is important to agree to clear lines of authority, accountability, and oversight for the position.

On a day-to-day basis, the priorities of the functional analyst should be set by the area to which they report. However, there should also be a mechanism, either through the SIS governance bodies or via the organizational structure of student services (if there is an overall leader for student services, for example), to assign the analyst to work on divisionwide priorities. Such a mechanism enables the staff to be pooled to work on major projects such as an upgrade or to help out if there is a growing backlog of work in another functional area.

Recruiting Functional Analysts. There is no single career path from which good functional analysts emerge. Some are former applications developers who have acquired deep understanding of one or more functional areas. Others are former frontline student services staff who, through work on an implementation project, have developed a working knowledge of technology in general and of the SIS in particular. Many are former SIS implementation consultants who are interested in a more stable work-life balance. Regardless of background, the essential skills of the functional analyst include the following:

- Effective communication
- Project management
- Process analysis
- Experience implementing SISs
- Ability to work independently
- Strong problem-solving skills

During the recruiting process for functional analysts, functional units should solicit the input of the administrative systems staff in central IT. They should provide input into the job descriptions of functional analysts and be included in the interview process. Once functional analysts are hired, they should be encouraged to work closely with the IT organization. They should be invited to attend administrative computing staff meetings (or meetings of the SIS support team). They should seek opportunities to join the IT staff in attending professional conferences and user-group meetings. Finally, functional areas should solicit the input of central IT when conducting performance evaluations on functional analysts.

Forging a close working relationship between IT staff and the functional analysts has two benefits. The primary benefit is, of course, a more productive and effective support team for the SIS. This relationship may also help the institution retain the functional analyst. Since there is no natural institutional career path for functional analysts, it is difficult to motivate and retain them through the promise of promotion. Rather, they may be motivated by the chance to learn new skills (and new technologies) and to participate in challenging projects. A close partnership with IT can help the student services organization provide its functional analysts with these opportunities.

Summary

Modern SISs offer many benefits in terms of enhanced functions that drive the improvement of services and increase access to information to support decision making. SISs are essential to many innovations in student services, such as self-service. In addition, the information captured by SISs provides vital data that can help institutions improve retention, spot trends in enrollment, and forecast demand for courses. However, these systems require a commitment that extends far beyond the initial implementation. During the planning and selection phases, institutions need to weigh carefully the total cost of owning and operating an SIS. Funding and staffing plans that acknowledge the continuous implementation effort these systems require need to be established for both IT and functional departments. A realistic plan for meeting this ongoing support challenge may in fact be more essential to realizing benefit from a technology investment than choosing the product with the most features.

Ongoing success also requires a new partnership between IT and student service functional offices. Functional areas must recognize and accept that they are co-owners of the system and must play an active role in its maintenance. IT organizations must accept this shared responsibility and cede to functional areas the authority they need to govern and maintain the system. Effective governance structures are needed to coordinate the many operational decisions that will arise as a byproduct of the integrated nature of modern SISs. These same governance groups must be empowered to make hard choices among numerous priorities for enhancement and among the scarce resources available to act on these priorities.

Finally, student service organizations need to change how they think about their staffing needs. They need to create positions like the functional analyst role that are dedicated both to managing the SIS and to extracting additional benefit from it. In this way, the institution will be in the best position to maximize the return on its investment in technology.

References

Goldstein, P. *Funding in Higher Education.* Boulder, Colo.: EDUCAUSE Center for Applied Research, 2004.

Kvavik, R., and Goldstein, P. *Good Enough! IT Investment and Business Process Performance in Higher Education.* Boulder, Colo.: EDUCAUSE Center for Applied Research, 2005.

Kvavik, R., and Katz, R. *The Promise and Performance of Enterprise Systems for Higher Education.* Boulder, Colo.: EDUCAUSE Center for Applied Research, 2002.

Powel, W., and Barry, J. "Planning for the Future by Looking Back." *EDUCAUSE Quarterly,* 2005, 3, 40–46.

PHILIP J. GOLDSTEIN *is an independent higher education consultant and research fellow with the EDUCAUSE Center for Applied Research. He has more than sixteen years of experience consulting with colleges and universities on the implementation and use of technology to improve administrative services.*

> The hidden dimensions of leadership and of the costs associated with the implementation of new information systems should be carefully considered. They can help determine the short- and long-term success of new systems.

The Impact of Implementing New Information Systems on the Priorities, Management, and Allocation of Resources at Colleges and Universities

Don Hossler

After reading the previous chapters it should be clear that the decision to implement a new student information system (SIS) is a complex, time-consuming, and costly undertaking. Whether implementing a vended system or developing a homegrown information system, there is far more for university administrators and faculty to consider than the costs of acquiring the software and hardware or the costs of developing a new homegrown system. In this final chapter I close with some observations and lessons learned for institutions implementing new information systems. Some of these lessons are close to the surface and easily visible, even to casual participants in new information system projects; others are subtle and less evident.

Systems Are Costly and Complicated Undertakings

During the period in which I helped lead the implementation of the PeopleSoft® SIS at Indiana University, I was often asked to meet with faculty governance groups. The most frequently recurring question I heard was, "Why do we have to do this and why does it cost so much?" Questions like this reflect the success that many universities have experienced in managing their SISs in the past. On most campuses, experienced functional and

technical managers have done their jobs well: they have made their systems work invisibly while providing services for faculty, students, and management. Not surprisingly, when faculty, administrators, and students are unhappy with their current systems, they are more likely to welcome the implementation of a new system as an opportunity to redress the significant limitations of the existing systems.

In response to the cost question often raised by faculty members, new systems are expensive for many reasons. Each year, the system expectations of various campus constituencies increase. For example, students desire more registration system services to be accessible at any time via the Web. Admissions staff want the recruitment system to provide increasingly customized communication with prospective students. Colleges are increasingly using Web-based advising systems because they are less costly and easier to update than paper file systems, and because they can be made available to students twenty-four hours a day. Similarly, faculty and staff expect the human resource system to provide users with unfettered online access to all employment and benefits information. Older vended or legacy systems often lacked these capacities, but new systems include these functions, which drive up the costs. In addition, faculty design increasingly sophisticated curricula or want academic programs to start and end at any time during the year. All of these functionalities require more complex and costly systems. In turn, these complex systems require technical staff with more education and specialized training. Individuals who possess the requisite technical and functional knowledge also command larger salaries.

New systems almost always result in the need to change campus business practices. These changes can create turmoil due to the costs associated with training and with the need to replace staff who are not enthusiastic about the changes. There is also the desire to have new systems redress all of the problems and shortcoming of previous systems. This is not surprising, because part of the business case typically made for replacing aging systems is that the new systems will solve many of the shortcomings of the existing systems. Efforts to address these shortcomings also result in additional costs to colleges and universities.

In the final analysis, there are no silver bullets; new systems and the changes that come with them are always expensive. Senior campus policymakers or middle managers involved in SIS implementations should be wary of budget plans for systems that promise significant savings over what peer institutions have spent. All too often, conversations I had with individuals involved with implementations around the country revealed a pattern of senior campus administrators who had little knowledge or experience with the systems that were going to be replaced yet had to come up with an implementation budget based on what they were willing to pay rather than a realistic assessment of what it would take to implement a usable system. Such plans are most likely unrealistic because they fail to include many of the costs discussed in this volume, ranging from required customizations, necessary backfill staff, consultants, and training to the ongoing expenses associated with hiring new staff with higher skill levels.

Multicampus Systems Make Implementation More Complicated

Multicampus institutions such as large community college systems or statewide university systems inevitably make information system implementations very visible and thus complicated. Each campus in a multicampus system is likely to have unique academic programs, specialized market niches, and differences in campus administration and governance that are reflected in the way administrators, faculty, staff, and students expect and desire their information systems to work. For example, different campuses within a university system often serve different types of students. The course-taking patterns, advising needs, and financial aid concerns of an eighteen-year-old, full-time, residential, first-year student and those of a thirty-two-year-old, part-time, commuting student with children are likely to be quite different from each other and may lead to genuine differences in the needs of the SISs that serve each of these populations.

At the same time, the system's president and other officers, such as the chief academic, financial, and information officers, are likely to want everything uniform across the system in order to hold down implementation costs. These tensions inevitably lead to conflicts. Not surprisingly, senior system administrators are advocates for noncustomized implementations across all campuses when planning an implementation initiative. However, when a senior system administrator discovers that a vanilla implementation means that one of his or her strongly held convictions regarding what the new system should do cannot in fact be done with the new system, then conflicts emerge. The more campuses there are in a multicampus system, the greater the likelihood that conflict will arise.

In addition, the bigger the multicampus system is, the more likely it is that the costs of implementation will become an easy target for criticism. Criticism can be expected because multicampus systems as well as trustees, legislators, and the media have a penchant for adding up the costs of similar activities across all of the institutions within the system. Thus an implementation that cost approximately $12 million at seven distinct and independent institutions becomes an $84 million project for a large multicampus system. Trustees, state legislators, and the media will inevitably pay more attention to an $84 million project that is having even the slightest problems than a smaller ($12 million project) at an individual campus. This confluence of issues inevitably makes multicampus implementations more complex and difficult than single-campus implementations.

Closely linked to the costs associated with the implementation of an ERP in a multicampus system is the timeline for implementation. If a plan does not provide for sufficient backfill and consulting, an aggressive timeline can create significant problems for implementation efforts. Each year that an implementation runs beyond the planned timeline increases the costs. The interaction of different campus budgets and timelines often plays a major role in determining the success of an ERP implementation. A realistic assessment of the hardware, software, staffing, consulting costs, and the time it will take to implement the system is critical to a successful multicampus system implementation.

The Impact of New Systems on Student Services

A quiet revolution is under way in many areas of student services, and new system implementations are accelerating the pace of these changes. In offices such as the bursar, comptroller, financial aid, and to some extent even admissions, the nature of the work and the expertise needed in these areas is changing. At the moment, most senior administrators and faculty are unaware of these trends and their implications.

Until recently, professionals were primarily subject-matter specialists who had great expertise in areas such as student financial aid regulations, course scheduling, or admissions communication functions. However, as computer-based information systems have become more sophisticated, professionals have also been asked to become as knowledgeable about technology (hardware, software, the Internet, and intranets) as they are about course scheduling or admissions standards. The interconnectedness of new SISs requires that all student service units have strong technology staffs and managers with knowledge of the relevant subject matter areas and of the functionalities of information systems to enable the work to get done.

The level of collaboration and cooperation required across many of these offices has also grown exponentially. In older information systems, many of these offices had separate systems that enabled each unit to work independently. Whether vended or homegrown, new information systems typically share many data elements, and the functionalities of the system across all of the offices are tightly linked. This interrelationship requires a considerable number of consultation and systems specialists who can manage the multiple and sometimes conflicting needs of these units.

These changes are producing two significant alterations in many student service units. One, these units are likely to find themselves becoming part of one reporting organization. There are efficiencies and wisdom in doing this. Even though all campus organizations want the best for the colleges and universities in which they are housed, they do not always agree on priorities. Thus there will always be clashes over resources and attention between functional offices and technology units. In this context, it is wise to have the needs of functional units articulated by a single vice president rather than by multiple and potentially conflicting voices.

In addition, campus administrators are discovering that the changing nature of student service professionals is bringing added staffing costs. Professionals with both subject matter and technology expertise are expensive. In addition, even support staffs are now required to have technology skills that raise the institution's salary costs. These trends are often not understood at the start of system implementations but they inevitably raise the associated staffing costs. I am not suggesting that these costs are avoidable; they are not, but they need to be included in the anticipated costs of implementing a new student system.

Working with the Faculty

It is axiomatic that most faculty will know little about the institution's legacy information systems. They are also likely to take little interest in new systems unless these systems affect them directly. Most of the changes in a new financial system or a new human resource system are unlikely to have much impact on faculty; hence the faculty are unlikely to care or even be aware that an implementation is taking place. But changes in a registration system, which is the repository of all faculty policies regarding general education and major requirements as well as grading policies, do affect faculty and *they will care*. When problems arise in implementations, they are likely to be related to issues such as grading policies, unique curricular designs that the new system may have difficulty accommodating, or how degree programs are structured. Support from and strong involvement of the campus registrar are always essential.

In addition to their attitudes toward academic policies, as the costs of implementation increase, faculty will be more likely to care because they will see these costs as taking away from investments in the academic mission of their programs. In institutions that have a tradition of strong faculty governance, it is imperative that system implementations include the involvement and leadership of individuals from the faculty who have strong ties to the faculty leadership. Ideally these should be individuals who have spent enough time at the institution to understand faculty norms and culture. This understanding helps in two ways. First, these faculty can identify problems in advance and help make sure that key faculty needs are adequately addressed during the implementation. In situations where the costs of addressing faculty concerns are simply too high, strong academic leaders can help explain the reasons for decisions in ways that are consistent with faculty beliefs and values.

Paying attention to these issues does not guarantee that large groups of faculty will never become concerned about aspects of an SIS implementation, but it will reduce the frequency with which problems arise. Failure to be proactive in working with the faculty can result in the development of latent resentment and hostility toward new information system implementations. If a major problem arises later that increases the costs of the implementation or produces results that are unacceptable to the faculty, it can lead to coalescence of this latent hostility, which in turn could result in a strong and visible negative public reaction to the new system.

Needs at the Top

Virtually every guide to system implementation notes the need for the involvement of senior management. Using such ubiquitous terms as *leadership team, executive management,* or *VP sponsors,* implementation guides call for such groups to be prepared to help make key decisions at every step of the implementation. As the scope and costs of a system implementation increase, the necessity of such a group increases.

However, one of the problems with relying on such a group is that campus executives often approach implementation projects with the belief that their role will be mostly symbolic and that they will not have to dedicate much time to understanding the complexities of new information systems. In addition, these are busy individuals with hectic schedules. Without careful planning, months might pass between meetings simply because the members of the leadership team might not be able to find a time on the calendar when they are all available. Such attitudes, if not altered quickly, are likely to make implementations more difficult and costly than necessary. The lack of knowledgeable and available senior leadership can cripple system implementations because large, costly, multifaceted problems can languish for months. During system implementations, the adage "time is money" is always true.

In addition, because a campus executive group may not be able to meet as often as needed, one person, and only one, should be authorized to make decisions about contested issues if the need arises. Asking committees comprising even senior middle managers to make decisions about contentious issues can lead to decision paralysis that slows implementation progress. When a senior executive group cannot gather to make a decision, an individual needs to be designated project leader to make decisions.

More Subtle Issues

Toward the end of my tenure in leading a major SIS implementation, some more subtle but important implications for college and university administrators and faculty became visible. These concerns are less tangible than the preceding concerns, but not unimportant.

As the use of technology becomes more pervasive in postsecondary education, issues of power, authority, and control are becoming more evident in several areas. As I have already asked, should it be the faculty or the capacities of the new vended software system that determine what is possible with respect to academic policies related to the learning outcomes associated with the curriculum?

Many student service areas were first established to serve faculty and students. As these functions have become technologized, the lines of control have become blurred and uncertain and the risk of goal displacement is ever present. By goal displacement I mean the tendency that arises in which the implementation project's goal slowly and subtly shifts from implementing needed transactions for a student service unit or a human resource office to simply getting the new system installed. It is possible for a professional from the information technology (IT) department to announce that a new system has been successfully installed or implemented while the registrar or bursar finds that the functionality needed is not yet working and it may be months before it does. It is also possible to implement a new SIS with a functional grading system component but to learn that the faculty are unhappy because they have discovered that the new grading component cannot report plusses and minuses or accommodate a recently approved innovative, competency-based grading system.

These issues can become quite pronounced with new systems and the desire to move all information systems into one unified technology platform. Typically the IT staff determines the unified platform for the new system. However, it is possible that functional experts in such areas as finance, human resources, or student services will determine that the system with the most functionality and greatest capability for benefiting students or accomplishing the academic mission has been developed on a different platform from the one supported by the IT staff. There are no easy answers to these situations, but there is a need for constant vigilance in this area to make sure that technology and new systems do not simply become goals unto themselves.

Finally, one area not to be overlooked is the hidden implications of vended or new systems that are being jointly developed by several colleges and universities. In this area, analogies can be made with deferred maintenance on brick and mortar buildings. Almost all colleges and universities have deferred maintenance problems. Problems with aging buildings exist not because campus decision makers are unaware of the needs in this area. In my experience, most campus administrators are very aware, but each year as they struggle to allocate resources among hiring more faculty, providing wage increases, purchasing more journal subscriptions, and maintaining buildings, deferred maintenance on buildings often loses out in the competition for scarce resources.

In the past, colleges and universities knew they had problems with aging, homegrown legacy systems, but as with aging buildings, other priorities were deemed more important. In the new world of vended systems, or systems that are jointly developed by several institutions, a good deal of discretion is removed from campus policymakers. In a sense, the needs of information systems automatically move to the top of the priority list in the competition for resources. When a vendor releases a new version and announces it will no longer support older versions of its software, or when a consortium of institutions makes a similar announcement, users of the software have no choice but to incur the costs of upgrading their systems. This often means that in the area of information systems the concept of deferred maintenance no longer exists; upgrades have to be undertaken regardless of other campus priorities. Ultimately this may be good, but there should be no illusions. In the increasingly tight fiscal environment in which most colleges and universities exist, decision makers have locked in some cost structures and on the margins have reduced their discretion to allocate resources to other areas of the institution such as academic programs, salaries, new laboratory facilities, and so forth. These issues are seldom discussed openly. Indeed, many senior campus policymakers are unaware of these implications when making decisions to acquire and implement new information systems.

In the past decade the development and implementation of new administrative information systems has become a dominant concern for many colleges and universities. The expectations of students, faculty, and staff for faster and more accessible services continue to increase at an exponential rate. Finding the right balance and managing the costs is likely to remain a pressing issue for most senior campus policymakers. In these areas, experienced and thoughtful leadership is a valuable commodity.

DON HOSSLER *is professor of educational leadership and policy studies and director of Projects on Academic Success at Indiana University–Bloomington, where he has also served as vice chancellor for enrollment services for eight years.*

INDEX

Acquisition costs, 23–24
Administrators: ERP executive sponsorship by, 37–38, 74; governance role of, 41; implications of information systems for, 74–76; information system roles by, 74; lack of familiarity with information systems by, 8. *See also* Faculty; IHE (institution of higher education)

Babey, E. R., 3, 21, 33
Backfill, 3, 22
Barry, J., 26, 53
Bendoly, E., 10
"Big bang" implementation strategy, 44
Budget. *See* ERP budgets
Build-your-own: definition of, 4; strengths and weaknesses of, 17–19
Business process reengineering, 47

Cabrini College, 58
California State (Cal State), 58, 59
Camp, J., 28
Campbell-Kelly, M., 9, 10
Chronicle of Higher Education, 7
Communication plan: as critical success factor, 40–41; definition of, 22
Computer-based resource management systems, 9–10
Consultants, 22
Cornell University, 30
Costs. *See* ERPs implementation costs
Critical success factors: communication planning, 40–41; executive sponsorship, 37–38; funding, 40; implementation methodology, 38; project scope, 39–40; project staffing, 38–39
Curphy, G. J., 17
Customization: definition of, 22; software, 29–30, 47–48

Daigle, S. L., 21
DeBlois, P. B., 21
Degree audit modules, 27
Dewey, B. I., 21
Drexel University, 58

EDUCAUSE Center for Applied Research (ECAR), 61, 62
EDUCAUSE Core Data Study (2004), 26, 28, 29, 30
EDUCAUSE Current Issues Committee, 21
EDUCAUSE Quarterly, 53
ERP baseline code, 30
ERP budgets: building, 27; as critical success factor, 40
ERP project strategies: "big bang" implementation, 44; business process reengineering, 47; design and programming, 47–48; development of project plan, 46; fit-gap assessment, 46; going live, 49–50; phased, 45; reporting, 48–49; rules of engagement for gap resolution, 46–47; system or multicampus, 45–46; testing, 48; transition to production, 49
ERP projects: budgets of, 27, 40; governance of, 41; scope of, 39–40; technology challenges of, 43–44
ERP staffing: costs associated with, 26; costs of training, 28–29; creating and organizing, 42–43; as critical success factor, 38–39; IT security officer, 31; management structure of, 42; system coordinator, 31
ERP vendors: in-house consulting provided by, 28; staff training provided by, 28–29. *See also* Vended solutions
ERPs (enterprise resource planning systems): building-your-own, 4, 17–19; definition of, 4, 7, 22; introduction to implementing, 1–6; legacy, 4, 19–20, 70; multicampus, 45–46, 58–59, 71–72; myths and realities of, 12–20; vended, 5, 14–17; Y2K impact on development of, 10–12. *See also* Information systems; Resource management systems; SIS (student information systems)
ERPs implementation: building and executing project plan, 41–50; critical success factors for, 37–41; leadership preparation for, 36–37; recent focus on, 7–8; strategies for, 44–50; of

77

student, 35–50; terminology associated with, 3–5, 22
ERPs implementation costs: acquisition, 23–24; adequate funding as critical success factor, 40; building budget for, 27; challenges of, 69–71; customization of software, 22, 29–30, 47–48; degree audit modules, 27; of multicampus, 71–72; ongoing to maintain SIS (student information systems), 53–54; overview of, 24–31; postimplementation, 31–32; software licensing fees, 22, 25; staffing, 26; terminology associated with, 22; training expenses, 28–29
Executive sponsorship, 37–38, 74

Faculty: governance role of, 41; implications of information systems for, 74–76; information system role of, 73–74; lack of familiarity with information systems by, 8. *See also* Administrators; IHE (institution of higher education)
Financials (or financial) system, 4
Fit-gap: assessment of, 46; definition of, 4; rules of engagement for gap resolution, 46–47. *See also* Gaps
FORTRAN, 14
Functional analysts: definition of, 4, 65; organizing, 66–67; recruiting, 67; role of the, 65–66
Functional managers, definition of, 4

Gaps: definition of, 4; rules for resolution of, 46–47. *See also* Fit-gap
Ginnett, R. C., 17
Go-live testing, 49–50
Goldstein, P. J., 3, 53, 62, 68
Gonzaga University, 26, 53
Good Enough! IT Investment and Business Process Performance study (ECAR), 62
Gorr, W., 7, 20
Governance: developing effective SIS, 56–58; multicampus SIS, 58–59; need for SIS, 55–56; project plan provisions for, 41
Green, K. C., 21
Greentree Gazette, 7

Hardware and infrastructure: definition of, 22; maintenance fees associated with, 25–26

Harrison, M. S., 17, 19
Hawkins, B. L., 26, 28, 29, 30
Homegrown, 4
Hossler, D., 1, 3, 6, 7, 20, 69, 76
HRMS (human resource management system), 4
Hughes, R. L., 17

IHE (institution of higher education): continuous SIS implementation impacts on, 54–67; demands for information systems by, 7; emergence of computer-based resource management systems for, 9–10; ERP implementation costs for, 21–32; implications of information systems for, 74–76; lack of familiarity with information systems by, 8. *See also* Administrators; Faculty
Implementation methodology, 38. *See also* ERPs implementation
Indiana University, 69
Information systems: costs and complications of undertaking, 69–71; demands for, 7; emergence of computer-based resource management systems, 9–10; impact on student services by, 72–73; implications of, 74–76; lack of knowledge by administrators/faculty with, 8; multicampus, 45–46, 58–59, 71–72; senior management role in, 74; SIS (student information systems), 35–50, 53–68, 72–73; working with faculty on, 73–74. *See also* ERPs (enterprise resource planning systems)
Interface, 4
IT (information technology) department: ERP responsibilities of, 54; SIS management responsibilities of, 62–64t; SIS shared responsibilities of, 64–65
IT security officer, 31

Katz, R. N., 26, 28, 29, 30, 31, 61
Koch, C., 28
Kuali collaboration, 35
Kvavik, R. B., 26, 28, 29, 30, 31, 61, 62

Leadership preparation, 36–37
Legacy systems: definition of, 4; strengths and weaknesses of, 19–20, 70
Licensing fees, 22, 25

McDevitt, D., 30
Mainframe computers (1960s), 9
Maintenance fees, 22
Methodologies, 4
Migration, 4
Modification, 4
Multicampus systems: complications/costs of implementing, 71–72; governance of SIS, 58–59; implementation strategies for, 45–46
Murphy, C., 28

Nicolich, R., 26, 28, 29, 30

Olsen, F., 30
Open source software, 5
Oracle's human resources application, 4, 27
Oroumchian, F., 19

Pape, S., 3, 6
Patches and fixes, 5
PeopleSoft, 30, 69
Phased implementation strategy, 45t
Porter, R., 3, 35, 51
Postimplementation costs, 31–32
Powel, W. D., 26, 53
Project scope, 39–40. *See also* ERP projects
Prototype, definition of, 5

Rahgozar, M., 19
Reporting strategies, 48–49
Resource management systems: demands for, 7; emergence of, 9–10; HRMS (human resource management system), 4; Y2K as impetus for change in, 10–12. *See also* ERPs (enterprise resource planning systems)
Rigelhof, R., 38
Rudy, J. A., 26, 28, 29, 30

Sakai collaboration, 35
SEVIS (Student and Exchange Visitor Information System), 44
Shadow system, 5
Siegel, P., 13
SIS (student information systems): altered traditional boundaries in management of, 62–64t; building and executing the project plan, 41–50; challenges of, 35–36, 69; continual operations improvement of, 59–62; critical success factors for, 37–41; definition of, 5; governance impact on institutions by, 55–59; impact on student services by, 72–73; leadership preparation for, 36–37; new working relationships in, 64–67; ongoing workload and costs to maintain, 53–54. *See also* ERPs (enterprise resource planning systems)
SIS (student information systems) governance: developing successful, 56–58; multicampus, 58–59; need for, 55–56
SIS (student information systems) improvement: practicing continuous, 61–62; small changes and big impacts of, 59–60; upgrades and, 60–61
SIS (student information systems) relationships: functional analyst role and, 65–66; organizing functional analysts, 66–67; recruiting functional analysts, 67; shared responsibilities through, 64–65
SIS (student information systems) responsibilities: change drivers of, 63; historical division of, 62; new division of roles and, 63–64t
Software: customization of, 22, 29–30, 47–48; definition of, 22; fit-gap issue of, 4, 46–47; licensing costs associated with, 22, 25; programming activities, 47–48; technology challenges of, 43–44; testing, 48; upgrading, 60–61
Soni, A., 10
State University of New York (SUNY), 58
Sullivan, L., 3, 35, 51
System coordinator, 31

Technical managers, 5
Technology challenges, 43–44
Testing: go-live, 49–50t; strategies for ERP, 48
Third-party products, 5

Universities. *See* IHE (institution of higher education)
University of Minnesota, 26
University of North Carolina, 58
Upgrades, 5

Vanilla, 5
Vended solutions: definition of, 5; strengths and weaknesses of, 14–17, 70. *See also* ERP vendors
Venkataramanan, M. A., 10

Walsh, B., 30
Walton, G. H., 17, 19
Web CT, 29
Web sites: Kuali collaboration, 35; Sakai collaboration, 35

West, R., 21
Workarounds, 5

Y2K problem, 10–12

Back Issue/Subscription Order Form

Copy or detach and send to:

Jossey-Bass, A Wiley Imprint, 989 Market Street, San Francisco CA 94103-1741
Call or fax toll-free: Phone 888-378-2537 6:30AM–3PM PST; Fax 888-481-2665

Back Issues: Please send me the following issues at $29 each.
(Important: please include series initials and issue number, such as HE114.)

_____

_____

_____

$ _____ Total for single issues

$ _____ Shipping charges: Surface   Domestic   Canadian
                              First item $5.00 $6.00
                              Each add'l item $3.00 $1.50

For next-day and second-day delivery rates, call the number listed above.

Subscriptions: Please ___ start ___ renew my subscription to *New Directions for Higher Education* for the year 2_____ at the following rate:

U.S.   ___ Individual $80   ___ Institutional $195
Canada   ___ Individual $80   ___ Institutional $235
All others   ___ Individual $104   ___ Institutional $269

Online subscriptions are available via Wiley InterScience!

For more information about online subscriptions visit www.wileyinterscience.com

$_____ Total single issues and subscriptions (Add appropriate sales tax for your state for single issue orders. No sales tax for U.S. subscriptions. Canadian residents, add GST for subscriptions and single issues.)

___ Payment enclosed (U.S. check or money order only)
___ VISA ___ MC ___ AmEx # _____ Exp. date _____

Signature _____ Day phone _____
___ Bill me (U.S. institutional orders only. Purchase order required.)

Purchase order # _____

Federal Tax ID13559302   GST 89102 8052

Name _____
Address _____
_____
Phone _____ E-mail _____

For more information about Jossey-Bass, visit our Web site at www.josseybass.com

Your guide to serving a new generation of students.

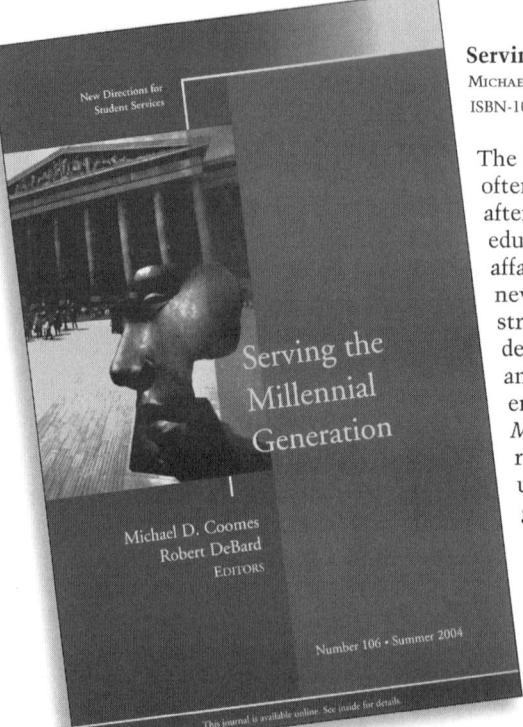

Serving the Millenial Generation
MICHAEL D. COOMES AND ROBERT DEBARD, EDITORS
ISBN-10: 0-7879-7606-7 • $28.00

The Millennial Generation, often categorized as those born after 1981, will require higher education leaders and student affairs practitioners to adopt new learning and service strategies, rethink student development theories, and modify educational environments. *Serving the Millennial Generation* gives readers the foundation for understanding this newest generation of students and to offer suggestions on how to educate and serve them more effectively.

Table of Contents:

1. **A Generational Approach to Understanding Students**
   MICHAEL D. COOMES AND ROBERT DEBARD

2. **Understanding the Historical and Cultural Influences That Shape Generations**
   MICHAEL D. COOMES

3. **Millennials Coming to College** ROBERT DEBARD

4. **Constructions of Student Development Across the Generations**
   C. CARNEY STRANGE

5. **Teaching, Learning, and Millennial Students**
   MAUREEN E. WILSON

6. **Understanding Diversity in Millennial Students**
   ELLEN M. BROIDO

7. **Student Affairs for a New Generation**
   JOHN WESLEY LOWERY

   Serving the Millennial Generation is a best-selling issue of the quarterly report *New Directions for Student Services*. Subscriptions can be ordered by calling 888-378-2537.

Order this title by calling 800-956-7739, or online at www.josseybass.com/go/ndss

Wiley, the Wiley logo, and the Jossey-Bass logo are trademarks or registered trademarks of John Wiley & Sons, Inc.

JOSSEY-BASS
An Imprint of WILEY
Now you know.

NEW DIRECTIONS FOR HIGHER EDUCATION IS NOW AVAILABLE ONLINE AT WILEY INTERSCIENCE

What is Wiley InterScience?

Wiley InterScience is the dynamic online content service from John Wiley & Sons delivering the full text of over 300 leading scientific, technical, medical, and professional journals, plus major reference works, the acclaimed *Current Protocols* laboratory manuals, and even the full text of select Wiley print books online.

What are some special features of Wiley InterScience?

Wiley InterScience Alerts is a service that delivers table of contents via e-mail for any journal available on Wiley InterScience as soon as a new issue is published online.
Early View is Wiley's exclusive service presenting individual articles online as soon as they are ready, even before the release of the compiled print issue. These articles are complete, peer-reviewed, and citable.
CrossRef is the innovative multi-publisher reference linking system enabling readers to move seamlessly from a reference in a journal article to the cited publication, typically located on a different server and published by a different publisher.

How can I access Wiley InterScience?

Visit http://www.interscience.wiley.com

Guest Users can browse Wiley InterScience for unrestricted access to journal Tables of Contents and Article Abstracts, or use the powerful search engine.
Registered Users are provided with a *Personal Home Page* to store and manage customized alerts, searches, and links to favorite journals and articles. Additionally, Registered Users can view free Online Sample Issues and preview selected material from major reference works.
Licensed Customers are entitled to access full-text journal articles in PDF, with select journals also offering full-text HTML.

How do I become an Authorized User?

Authorized Users are individuals authorized by a paying Customer to have access to the journals in Wiley InterScience. For example, a university that subscribes to Wiley journals is considered to be the Customer. Faculty, staff and students authorized by the university to have access to those journals in Wiley InterScience are Authorized Users. Users should contact their Library for information on which Wiley journals they have access to in Wiley InterScience.

ASK YOUR INSTITUTION ABOUT WILEY INTERSCIENCE TODAY!

United States Postal Service
Statement of Ownership, Management, and Circulation

1. Publication Title	2. Publication Number	3. Filing Date
New Directions For Higher Education	0 2 7 1 – 0 5 6 0	10/1/06

4. Issue Frequency	5. Number of Issues Published Annually	6. Annual Subscription Price
Quarterly	4	$195.00

7. Complete Mailing Address of Known Office of Publication *(Not printer) (Street, city, county, state, and ZIP+4)*	Contact Person
Wiley Subscription Services, Inc. at Jossey-Bass, 989 Market Street, San Francisco, CA 94103	Joe Schuman
	Telephone (415) 782-3232

8. Complete Mailing Address of Headquarters or General Business Office of Publisher *(Not printer)*

Wiley Subscription Services, Inc. 111 River Street, Hoboken, NJ 07030

9. Full Names and Complete Mailing Addresses of Publisher, Editor, and Managing Editor *(Do not leave blank)*

Publisher *(Name and complete mailing address)*

Wiley Subscriptions Services, Inc., A Wiley Company at San Francisco, 989 Market Street, San Francisco, CA 94103-1741

Editor *(Name and complete mailing address)*

Martin Kramer, 2807 Shasta Road, Berkeley, CA 94708

Managing Editor *(Name and complete mailing address)*

None

10. Owner *(Do not leave blank. If the publication is owned by a corporation, give the name and address of the corporation immediately followed by the names and addresses of all stockholders owning or holding 1 percent or more of the total amount of stock. If not owned by a corporation, give the names and addresses of the individual owners. If owned by a partnership or other unincorporated firm, give its name and address as well as those of each individual owner. If the publication is published by a nonprofit organization, give its name and address.)*

Full Name	Complete Mailing Address
Wiley Subscription Services, Inc.	111 River Street, Hoboken, NJ 07030
(see attached list)	

11. Known Bondholders, Mortgagees, and Other Security Holders Owning or Holding 1 Percent or More of Total Amount of Bonds, Mortgages, or Other Securities. If none, check box ➤ ☑ None

Full Name	Complete Mailing Address
None	None

12. Tax Status *(For completion by nonprofit organizations authorized to mail at nonprofit rates) (Check one)*
The purpose, function, and nonprofit status of this organization and the exempt status for federal income tax purposes:
☐ Has Not Changed During Preceding 12 Months
☐ Has Changed During Preceding 12 Months *(Publisher must submit explanation of change with this statement)*

13. Publication Title: New Directions For Higher Education
14. Issue Date for Circulation Data Below: Summer 2006

15. Extent and Nature of Circulation		Average No. Copies Each Issue During Preceding 12 Months	No. Copies of Single Issue Published Nearest to Filing Date
a. Total Number of Copies *(Net press run)*		1403	1277
b. Paid and/or Requested Circulation	(1) Paid/Requested Outside-County Mail Subscriptions Stated on Form 3541. *(Include advertiser's proof and exchange copies)*	735	682
	(2) Paid In-County Subscriptions Stated on Form 3541 *(Include advertiser's proof and exchange copies)*	0	0
	(3) Sales Through Dealers and Carriers, Street Vendors, Counter Sales, and Other Non-USPS Paid Distribution	0	0
	(4) Other Classes Mailed Through the USPS	0	0
c. Total Paid and/or Requested Circulation *[Sum of 15b. (1), (2),(3),and (4)]* ➤		735	682
d. Free Distribution by Mail *(Samples, complimentary, and other free)*	(1) Outside-County as Stated on Form 3541	0	0
	(2) In-County as Stated on Form 3541	0	0
	(3) Other Classes Mailed Through the USPS	0	0
e. Free Distribution Outside the Mail *(Carriers or other means)*		67	67
f. Total Free Distribution *(Sum of 15d. and 15e.)* ➤		67	67
g. Total Distribution *(Sum of 15c. and 15f)* ➤		802	749
h. Copies not Distributed		601	528
i. Total *(Sum of 15g. and h.)* ➤		1403	1277
j. Percent Paid and/or Requested Circulation *(15c. divided by 15g. times 100)*		92%	91%

16. Publication of Statement of Ownership
☑ Publication required. Will be printed in the Winter 2006 issue of this publication. ☐ Publication not required.

17. Signature and Title of Editor, Publisher, Business Manager, or Owner: Susan E. Lewis, VP & Publisher - Periodicals   Date: 10/01/06

I certify that all information furnished on this form is true and complete. I understand that anyone who furnishes false or misleading information on this form or who omits material or information requested on the form may be subject to criminal sanctions (including fines and imprisonment) and/or civil sanctions (including civil penalties).